UPSTAGING GOD

∽ Pelle Karlsson ∾

WORD PUBLISHING

Dallas•London•Vancouver•Melbourne

Library of Congress Cataloging-in-Publication Data
Karlsson, Pelle, 1950–
Upstaging God : restoring superstar status to
Jesus alone / Pelle Karlsson.
p. cm.
ISBN 0-8499-3955-0
1. Jesus Christ—Lordship. 2. Church. I. Title
BT205.K37   1996
232—dc20
96-393 CIP

Printed in the United States of America
6 7 8 9 RRD 9 8 7 6 5 4 3 2 1

CONTENTS

Chapter 4   SPIRITUAL LEADERSHIP

Chapter 5   IN HIS NAME

INTRODUCTION

The great teacher in the New Covenant is the Holy Spirit. The role of man is only to put into words and emphasize that which the Holy Spirit is already communicating to everyone who would listen. So, when introduced to any teaching in spoken or written form—including these pages—receive only that which the Holy Spirit confirms in your heart. He is the teacher and we are His students, not the students of any man or man-made system. Remember that Jesus said: *"All this I have spoken while still with you. But the Counselor, the Holy Spirit, whom the Father will send in My name, will teach you all things and will remind you of everything I have said to you"* (John 14:25–26). No man can ever assume this role or in any way substitute for the Holy Spirit. No human being—no matter who it is—has a complete understanding of the whole truth. Only the Spirit is able to communicate the full truth, using various ways to speak to us.

Trust the work of the Holy Spirit in your heart. Trust also in your own ability to hear from God through His Spirit. This ability is part of the new man created within you through the work of Christ. If exercised correctly, it will lead to greater spiritual maturity.

⌒ Chapter 1 ⌒
THE ORIGINAL SIN

Infiltration

It appears that the Church now frequently uses expressions like "VIPs," "celebrities," "stars," "heroes," "super pastors," "top singers," "popular speakers," etc., as part of its regular life. All of which is basically unscriptural! And even if such obvious labels are not directly involved, undue focus is still often placed on people in spiritual leadership, since they are sometimes seen as "significant" and "prominent." In this teaching, we choose to define this phenomenon as the attention-on-man syndrome. We will attempt to explore this syndrome and show that it has a severe impact on the effectiveness of the Church in the spiritual battle. Indeed, it has led the Christian community into many unnecessary situations of defeat, because it is often much neglected and misunderstood.

But why couldn't we at least accept a "moderate" level of VIPs and celebrities in the Church? After all, this is the earth—not heaven! Simply because there aren't any human celebrities or "significant" people in the work of God. Not locally, not nationally, not internationally. The Apostle Paul makes a powerful statement to that effect when he addresses the Corinthians regarding their tendency to put some leaders above others. "*What, after all, is Apollos? And what is Paul? Only servants, through whom you came to believe—as the Lord has assigned to each his task. I planted the seed, Apollos watered it, but God made it grow. **So neither he who plants nor he who waters is anything, but only God, who makes things grow**" (1 Cor. 3:5–7, bolded by author). This is a fundamental truth in Scripture. No matter what man does or whatever level of visibility he might have been given in the Church— man in himself is of no significance in the work of God. All performance comes from the Lord without whom we would all be unable to achieve anything of spiritual value. The attention-on-man syndrome however, tends to always indicate the opposite—that certain people are really "something" and should be given great attention. This idea is completely contrary to the very heart of the Kingdom of God and will do damage if given a foothold. Frankly, the overemphasized focus on man's role in God's work has become so prevalent that the following call might have to be issued: LET'S GIVE THE CHURCH BACK TO THE LORD! Not that we can actually take it from Him. But unless we get our priorities straight here, we will not truly become the living stones by which He can build His house.

The comprehension of this area, as well as other areas of spiritual warfare, is essential for the Church's ability to correctly apply Christ's victory in this world. As our spiritual understanding grows, so does our effectiveness to battle the enemy. Not because we gain more power in ourselves, but because we see the power and strength of the Lord and discover His ability to assert His victory through the Church.

First, we need to look at a certain strategy often used in warfare: infiltration. In any war, it is desirable for the contending parties to try to infiltrate each other in order to gain advantage. To infiltrate means to penetrate weaknesses in the enemy lines in order to attack or try to seize control from within. Infiltration is often done in secrecy with an attempt to hide what is actually going on. No one is supposed to know that the enemy is present within and possibly has gained access to high level posts. If one party is successful in infiltrating the other, that party can immediately create suspicion, mistrust, division and defeat on the other side.

It works the same in the spiritual realm. Satan constantly tries to infiltrate the Church, God's army on earth, in order to divide and conquer. He relentlessly looks for weaknesses in the battle lines so that he may attempt to infiltrate and work from within. Like in any other war, he tries to do this in secrecy without being detected and uncovered in his plans. His method is that of a secret agent using false names, false identification papers, disguises, lies, and deceit in order to accomplish infiltration.

The Apostle Paul warns the Corinthians about this method of operation by the devil. *"Satan himself masquerades as an angel of light"* (2 Cor. 11:14). In Ephesians 4, Paul also urges the Church to speak truthfully, to watch out for anger, bitterness, rage, slander, etc. He then states very clearly: *". . . do not give the devil a foothold"* (Eph. 4:27). In other words, we must watch out for that which is common behavior among man; anger, slander, etc., or the devil will immediately infiltrate and gain a foothold. Paul makes it very clear as well, that this is the arena where the real battle is taking place. *"Put on the full armor of God so that you can take your stand against the devil's schemes. For our struggle is not against flesh and blood, but against the rulers, against the authorities, against the powers of this dark world and against the forces of evil in the heavenly realms"* (Eph. 6:11–12).

Satan is continuously scheming and plotting for ways to infiltrate the Church, to discredit the Word of God and to hinder His plan. A quite dramatic example of this is found in Matthew 16. First, Simon Peter makes a strong confession regarding Jesus as the Son of God: *"You are the Christ, the Son of the living God.' Jesus replied, 'Blessed are you, Simon son of Jonah, for this was not revealed to you by man, but by My Father in heaven. And I tell you that you are Peter, and on this rock I will build My Church,*

and the gates of Hades will not overcome it." (Matt. 16:16–18).
Then, the Scripture continues: *"From that time on Jesus began to explain to His disciples that He must go to Jerusalem and suffer many things at the hands of the elders, chief priests and teachers of the law, and that He must be killed and on the third day be raised to life. Peter took Him aside and began to rebuke Him. 'Never, Lord!' he said. 'This shall never happen to you!' Jesus turned and said to Peter, 'Out of my sight, Satan! You are a stumbling block to Me; you do not have in mind the things of God, but the things of men."* (Matt. 16:21–23).

How is it that a man that has just been blessed by Jesus for his revelation knowledge and spiritual understanding, suddenly is rebuked as an instrument of Satan? The explanation is quite simple. Due to lack of understanding on Peter's part as to how God was to establish Jesus in His Lordship, (i.e. through death on the cross), Peter wanted to be kind and compassionate and protect Jesus from any harm. Well, human goodness and compassion don't always cut it in the Kingdom of God! Only the perfect will of God can accomplish a spiritual work. Satan found an open door and immediately tried to infiltrate the situation. Note that Jesus turned to Peter, but actually spoke to Satan. Peter wasn't Satan, but Satan had used Peter's human "goodness" to oppose the plan of God. That is why Jesus firmly identified this thought as the things of men and not the things of God. However, had Jesus not been there to quickly de-mask the infiltration attempt by the enemy, this idea would have remained as a valid option in the minds of Peter and others.

Target Area

We will now specifically focus on the attention-on-man syndrome, by which it seems that Satan has been able to strongly infiltrate the Church. The issue of man's position in God's work has always been a target for the enemy and certainly is a major area of assault in our time. In words we often hear that the Church should be filled with nothing but humble servants, and that leaders should be seen only as instruments in the hand of Christ. Not as something powerful in themselves. But in practical reality, both from the perspective of the shepherds as well as the perspective of the flock, it isn't always so. Christians are often quite confused regarding how to apply and receive leadership. And Satan is always ready to take advantage of this.

The first thing we will notice when we look closer at the attention-on-man syndrome is the great similarity between the Church and the entertainment industry in this respect. In the entertainment world one is looking for the "hottest" name and the most famous star in order to make a project successful. Unfortunately, the same holds true for the Church many times. We create Christian events, using the "hottest" names in order to succeed. This is not to say that those who can draw Christian crowds together are not true servants of God and cannot be used by Him. But we are attempting to show that the enemy has in this area infiltrated the Church and created a system which is basically paralyzing rather than bringing freedom to God's people.

Incidentally, it appears that the entertainment industry itself was created by Satan in order to bring joy and excitement to people while leaving out God, the true source of joy and inspiration. It is therefore no wonder that if we pattern ourselves after this, we will be hindered rather than helped in our attempt to serve in the Kingdom. It has become a common misunderstanding among God's people that if the Church has famous men and women just like the world, who can make good headlines and appear on the evening news, God's Kingdom is greatly helped. It is almost as if we have made God dependent on our strength rather than accepting the fact that His strength is manifested in our weakness.

Everywhere you look where the principles of God's strength versus man's weakness are not understood, you will find people looking for heroes. Either to become one themselves or to find one to look up to. This must never be the attitude in the Church, since it will hinder the true Lordship of Jesus Christ. Only Jesus has the right to that kind of attention. ". . . *He raised Him from the dead and seated Him at His right hand in the heavenly realms, far above all rule and authority, power and dominion, and every title that can be given, not only in the present age but also in the one to come. And God placed all things under His feet and appointed Him to be Head over everything for the Church, which is His Body, the fullness of Him who fills everything in every way* " (Eph. 1:20–23).

The Lucifer Connection

"*How you have fallen from heaven, O morning star, (Lucifer), son of the dawn! You have been cast down to the earth, you who once laid low the nations! You said in your heart, 'I will ascend to heaven; I will raise my throne above the stars of God; I will sit enthroned on the mount of assembly, on the utmost heights of the sacred mountain. I will ascend above the tops of the clouds; I will make myself like the Most High.' But you are brought down to the grave, to the depths of the pit*" (Isa. 14:12–15). This passage about the king of Babylon is also widely held to be an account of the fall of Satan. He, at first an angel of light, was thrown out of heaven and became God's greatest enemy. When Jesus once spoke to His disciples, He stated: "*I saw Satan fall like lightning from heaven*" (*Luke* 10:18). It is likely that Jesus here is giving an eyewitness report of this most remarkable event in eternal history.

What was it that made an angel of light be stripped of all his glory, cast down from his position, and turned into a vicious opponent of the One he had once served? Isaiah chapter 14 makes it clear. It was pride, desire for power, desire for glory, and desire to be exalted with full attention on himself that resulted in his downfall. That's why he was thrown from heaven like fireworks. This is the original sin. Satan tries to have this sin repeated over and over again among mankind. He knows, after his own tumultuous experience by having his hunger for power and glory dashed by a righteous God who could not tolerate that kind of an attitude, that this is the way to destroy God's work and plan for individuals and for the Church collectively. If he can get Christians caught in the attention-on-man syndrome, either by exalting themselves or exalting others, God's plan and purpose will be hindered. There is no place for personal ambition or attention on man in the workings of the Most High. When this occurs, it is not part of the Kingdom, and God may have to hold back His work even among those who once were called and dedicated to true service. Satan knows this well and is therefore constantly attempting to infiltrate the Church in this area. His own experience tells him that this is an effective way to oppose God's Kingdom.

Interestingly, while yet an angel of light, so strong was this desire within Lucifer that although he wanted to be *"like the Most High,"* he could not see that this very attitude was totally unacceptable to God and would completely prevent any possibility to actually be like the Most High. He was blinded by impure motives. Lucifer desired to be like the Most High, not to be righteous and holy like Him but rather to have power and glory like Him. This is a common attitude within the Church also. Sometimes, all the religious words and motions are used, yet not with pure motives to see the Kingdom of God established in the world but rather to gain glory, recognition, personal gain, or whatever. The words and actions may be just about identical but the spiritual reality is worlds apart. The Church must wake up and receive discernment in this area. The attention-on-man syndrome must be dealt with so that Lucifer no longer is allowed to infiltrate and terrorize the Church in this way.

Symptoms

The symptoms of the attention-on-man syndrome are fairly obvious and easy to detect. As soon as we encounter—either in plain sight or between the lines—expressions like "big names," "VIPs," "celebrities," "stars," "success stories," "super pastors," "famous evangelists," "top singers," "best-seller authors," "successful ministers," etc., we can expect that infiltration with this syndrome is either attempted or has already taken place. When focus is placed on popularity, status, ability or perceived position of any person in the Church, we should immediately be aware that there might be ulterior motives somewhere in the situation. Either by the VIP himself, or by those who have made him one in their minds. This is where infiltration takes place. Satan has found many open doors to the Church through this attitude. The attention-on-man syndrome creates a perfect breeding ground for demonic diversion with all the religious words and motions, but without the true power and purpose of God. And frankly, isn't this where the Church is at many times? An abundance of words and religious motions but little true spiritual authority and power.

It is quite possible that the world, especially the secular press, will call out VIPs among Christians, not knowing the workings of the Kingdom of God. But the Church itself must never fall for this behavior. God never has and never will make provisions for big names or celebrities in His work. He has always called men and women as humble servants. Granted, some with a bigger job on a more visible level from an earthly perspective. But everyone is of equal value in His eyes and every job is equally important. He never looks to His servants for performance and success as the world would. He only looks for obedience and humility of heart. A true servant of God, who has received this eternal perspective, can therefore never allow himself to become a VIP either in his own eyes or in anybody else's.

The Church is called to walk in the truth of God. Unless we are able to de-mask and withstand this area of Satanic infiltration, we will not be able to walk in full truth. We are dealing here with a foundational principle in the Kingdom of God. There is only One who has achieved celebrity status in the Kingdom—the bright Morning Star Himself! He has received God's full attention, has been given all authority in heaven and on earth, has been given a name and a title above every name in this age and in the age to come. He is now seated at the right hand of the Father, as the One worthy of any and all glory forever and ever. He, and only He, is to receive all attention in the Church.

This brings us to God's "status scale" for the Church. It is very simple. Jesus Christ (together with the Father and the Spirit) is number one—everyone else is number two! Let's receive this simple truth through the Spirit. It is an antidote for an anemic Church in the end times.

Change the Trend

It is time to start changing the trend and to adjust the course away from the attention-on-man syndrome which unfortunately, little by little, has become the norm within the Church. Modern humanistic philosophies are placing man more and more in the center without the need for God. And even if religion is involved, these philosophies still serve to bolster the confidence in man's own ability as the real strength. The world maintains that man in his own intelligence is able to address his own problems. We will find everything from the "You are your own god" theory to the simple view that normal, decent behavior will cure mankind's problems. All this bypasses God and puts the focus on man.

The Church must never fall prey to this kind of thinking. It must never look to the attributes of man; intelligence, eloquence of speech, charm, perceived high position, musical talent, leadership abilities—not even great abilities to memorize Scripture and spiritual theories—as something to be focused on. All this, even if exercised in great sincerity, can take the focus off the only One who is to be focused on—Jesus Christ. Remember how the Apostle Paul, a man with great capacity to "show off" if he had wanted to, approached the Corinthians: *"When I came to you, brothers, I did not come with eloquence or superior wisdom as I proclaimed to you the testimony about God. For I resolved to know nothing while I was with you except Jesus Christ and Him crucified. I came to you in weakness and fear, and with much trembling. My message and my preaching were not with wise and persuasive words, but with a demonstration of the Spirit's power, so that your faith might not rest on men's wisdom, but on God's power "* (1 Cor. 2:1–5). The Apostle Paul deliberately de-emphasized his human strengths in order for Christ to take center stage. This is not to say that God does not use human beings with special abilities. But if the spotlight fully or partially ends up on them and their abilities, either in their own eyes or others', something has gone very wrong. When God uses human beings to proclaim His word and to speak in His name, it is always for the purpose of placing focus on Jesus. Then, He is totally free to accomplish His work. Otherwise we might simply be fooling ourselves.

A change of the trend in this area is badly needed, since the attention-on-man syndrome also is a major contributor to the lack of understanding of God's will within the Church. When the Apostle Paul addresses the Romans, urging them to offer themselves as living sacrifices to God, he also states: *"Do not conform any longer to the pattern of this world, but be transformed by the renewing of your mind. Then you will be able to test and approve what God's will is—His good, pleasing and perfect will "* (Rom. 12:2). Paul then continues in this chapter to discuss man's position in God's work, based on the pattern of God and a renewed mind to understand God's will. He strongly underlines that we are all members of one Body, and of equal importance for its function under the Head. This is the pattern which is to prevail in the Church. The pattern of this world, on the other hand, is to focus on "special" people and make them the final point of attention. For those who do not see the risen Lord in his glory, man becomes the ultimate focal point. If we conform to this pattern, fully or partially, a serious situation will occur: We will not be able to discern the perfect will of God since our spiritual understanding will be clouded.

The Church is often running around in circles, like someone trying to find his way out of a maze, because we have not clearly understood God's will and plan for our current situation. The attention-on-man syndrome has put a veil over our spiritual eyes so that we have not been *"able to test and approve what God's will is."* This syndrome is a major part of the pattern of the world and, if allowed to prevail, will keep the Church in the dark as far as spiritual discernment and understanding is concerned. This is of course exactly what the enemy aims for when he tries to infiltrate the Church in this way. Therefore, as Paul states to the Romans: *"be transformed by the renewing of your mind."* We must think differently than the world or we will not be able to correctly discern God's will. This is essential for today's Church and the only basis for God to implement His specific plan in our time.

We truly need a drastic change of the trend in this area. Anyone who has entered the Church scene in a leadership position with any percentage of desire for recognition of himself, needs to repent. And God's people, so fixated with who is behind the pulpit, must start to look away from the instruments God is using in His Kingdom. Any other attitude will only promote the infiltration of the enemy, put a shadow on the correct view of Jesus, prevent us from truly understanding God's will and thereby severely hinder the Lord from doing His perfect work through the Church. It is impossible to have a full and correct view of Jesus and at the same time look at man according to the pattern of this world. Only if we focus totally on the Lord and not be concerned with whomever He may use at whatever level in His Kingdom, be it ourselves or others, can the Church stand up and show some spiritual muscle in the end times.

‿‿ Chapter 2 ‿‿
THE GREATEST

John the Baptist

Man's role in God's work is unique. We have quite a case study of a "great" servant of the Lord in John the Baptist. "*As John's disciples were leaving, Jesus began to speak to the crowd about John: 'What did you go out into the desert to see? A reed swayed by the wind? If not, what did you go out to see? A man dressed in fine clothes? No, those who wear fine clothes are in king's palaces. Then what did you go out to see? A prophet? Yes, I tell you, and more than a prophet. This is the one about whom it is written: "I will send My messenger ahead of You, who will prepare the way before You." I tell you the truth: Among those born of women there has not risen anyone greater than John the Baptist; yet he who is least in the Kingdom of heaven is greater than he'*" (Matt. 11:7–11).

John the Baptist had a peculiar mission right on the edge between the Old and the New Covenant. His life was specifically designed by God to fulfill this mission. Jesus speaks very powerful words about him: "*Among those born of women there has not risen anyone greater than John the Baptist."* It is interesting, by the way, that Jesus who Himself was born of a woman on earth, had no problems with calling John the greatest. Those that are truly great in heart can give full credit to others, while those who have a carnal desire for "greatness" will always see others as competition. Remember though that Jesus was brought forth as a baby by Mary but was really born by the Holy Spirit. *"This is how the birth of Jesus Christ came about. His mother Mary was pledged to be married to Joseph, but before they came together, she was found to be with child through the Holy Spirit "* (Matt. 1:18). Yes, Jesus was carried by Mary, as a surrogate mother if you will, but was supernaturally born by the Spirit. That is why He later gives a quite interesting answer to a crowd of people. *"A crowd was sitting around Him, and they told Him, 'Your mother and brothers are outside looking for You.' 'Who are My mother and My brothers?' He asked. Then He looked at those seated in a circle around Him and said, 'Here are My mother and My brothers! Whoever does God's will is My brother and sister and mother'"* (Mark 3:32–34). God had chosen Mary to bear Jesus as a baby, but He was not really "born of women" in the same sense as others. Thus, Jesus could say about John that he was the greatest born of women.

Did the word get back to John that Jesus had labeled him as the greatest? Perhaps. However, Jesus made the evaluation of John after John's disciples had left. He sent them back to the prison cell with the message of what He had done—not the evaluation of John as a servant which He later gave to the crowd of people. The perspective of one's own "status" in the Kingdom of God, i.e. effectiveness of service, perception by others, glory and attention to oneself, etc., is always a sensitive area among men and women in God's work. A wrongful attention here, even among the most "spiritual" ones, can trigger the old Lucifer-attitude and totally destroy God's plan for someone's life. Is it possible that Jesus did not send this specific message back to John's cell for that very reason, but rather focused on His own mighty works? One would think that a "You are the greatest" word from Jesus would have been of tremendous encouragement to the distraught John in his prison cell. But that's not the way it works in God's Kingdom.

By the way, it is very interesting to note that Jesus did not save the life of the *"greatest born of women."* As you may recall, Herodias' daughter had danced for Herod on his birthday, likely in a suggestive way, and he promised to give her anything she asked for. Because of the sinful behavior in that family, the request was made for John the Baptist's head on a platter. Talk about dirty dancing! Could Jesus have saved John from being beheaded by Herod? Of course! But He didn't. And neither did Jesus save His own life. For true servants of God, like Jesus in His earthly ministry, John, and many others, the main concern is not the comfort and safety of life. It is to speak the truth and do the will of God at any price. This is what creates greatness in the Kingdom of God.

What are We Looking for?

Jesus poses an interesting question when He speaks to the crowd about John the Baptist. *"What did you go out into the desert to see?"* (Matt. 11:7). Whenever God's word is communicated there are circumstances, situations, and people involved that might catch our eye. It is very easy to become focused on the method of communication or more particularly the communicator, instead of the message itself. There was much that could catch the eye in the work of John. Jesus asked the people what they expected to see: *"A reed swayed by the wind?"* John the Baptist most certainly looked like a reed in the wind in his seclusive existence in the barren desert. Most likely he was far from any barber shop and his hair might have been long and completely void of any hair spray, (unlike many of today's preachers!), flying wildly in the desert wind. His diet was that of grasshoppers and wild honey, low in fat and cholesterol. He probably looked very much like a reed in the wind, without any need to attend local exercise clubs to stay fit and slim. And in order to be "A *voice of one calling in the desert*" to the growing crowds, he may have spoken loud and forcefully. Quite a show for those who wanted to see a different individual. Lifestyles of the strange and blameless!

Jesus continues to ask them if they went out to see "A *man dressed in fine clothes?*" The Jerusalem fashion experts might have been puzzled. "*John's clothes were made of camel's hair, and he had a leather belt around his waist*" (Matt. 3:4). Would the fashion designers dare to create a new line of camelhair jeans with desert rat leather belt to capitalize on John's popularity among the crowds? This was certainly a rugged look that could be the thing of the future. Had they paid closer attention, however, they would have understood that this was nothing new. In 2 Kings, King Ahaziah had had an accident and turned to pagan gods regarding the situation. God then instructed the prophet Elijah to rebuke the king, and Elijah gave the word to the king's messengers. When the messengers returned, King Ahaziah asked them: "'*What kind of man was this who came to meet you and told you this?' They replied, 'He was a man with a garment of hair and a leather belt around his waist.' The king said, 'That was Elijah the Tishbite'*" (2 Kings 1:7–8). Interestingly, the king did not identify the prophet Elijah by the word that was spoken through him. One would think that Ahaziah could have done so simply by looking at his own situation in light of this prophetic word, knowing that Elijah was a prophet of God. But he immediately recognized the prophet when they described his clothing, the same style as John the Baptist wore. Unfortunately, there has always been a tendency to focus more on style, outward appearance, and circumstances rather than the Word of God itself.

Jesus continues His recollection of John. *"No, those who wear fine clothes are in king's palaces."* Without carrying this too far, there is a lesson of modesty here. The Church should not be a showplace for the hottest new thing in appearance, style, celebrities, music, clothing, or anything else like that. Any such focus will immediately take the focus off the Lord and His word and do damage to the Kingdom of God. Like Jesus said, if you want to see fine clothes, go to the palaces and the fancy places of the world. Don't come here!

Many probably showed up at John the Baptist's sermons just to have a look at this strange man in the desert. But unless they learned to re-focus from the appearance of John to the message he spoke, which many did and repented, they would have come in vain. The same holds true for the Church today. Unless we learn to deal with the attention-on-man syndrome, we will simply have a lot of action and reaction with little or no real spiritual value.

Jesus continues. *"Then what did you go out to see? A prophet? Yes, I tell you, and more than a prophet."* This is where Jesus places the emphasis. John looked and acted in a way that could grab the headlines. But that was incidental. The important thing about him was his call as a prophet, speaking a word from God to the people. What is so special about a prophet? His own abilities, style, clothes or whatever? Of course not. The only thing of importance is the One who has sent him and the message he was given to speak. John was not placed in the desert to draw attention to himself and to break some sand-dune attendance records. He was there to announce the work of God. *"I will send My messenger ahead of You."* We repeat again because of the extreme importance of this understanding: The special thing in this situation was not the messenger, but who had sent him and the reason why.

The only point worth attention in the work of John the Baptist was the call to repentance based on the fact that the Father was sending the Son to save the world from sin. John happened to be picked as a messenger to make some important announcements at a crucial time in the plan of God. But his desert style, rugged clothing, tone of voice or whatever, was of no significance. Only the message that God had chosen him to bring.

The question must also be asked of the Church today. What do we go out to see? What is the focus when we gather in church services, conferences, concerts, seminars, prayer groups, home fellowships, etc.? Is it to see Jesus only and to hear His word alone? Or have we become unduly occupied with the style and attributes of the men and women He has chosen as messengers? Are we "hooked" on the pure Word of God or on the messenger's speaking ability, style, looks, gimmicks, musical talents, theatrical behavior, or whatever else might attract a crowd?

These are extremely important issues which determine the level of spirituality in the Church. It seems that there often is an overemphasized importance put on the messengers. If we have a "hot" speaker or singer we can fill churches and auditoriums to the brim. On the other hand, if we advertise a gathering with Jesus as the only feature—the prayer meeting—we probably won't need to worry about enough parking spaces and room for the overflow crowds. Please, understand that we are not saying that it would be wrong for somebody to be known to carry a word from God and thereby able to attract the crowds. This is what John the Baptist did. But there is a fine line where the focus switches from the One who inspired the message to the messenger who brings it.

It is complete heresy to think that if we create excitement around God's messengers and elevate them to some VIP level, God's Kingdom is helped. Remember, His strength is manifested in our weakness—not the other way around. And the attention-on-man syndrome does major damage to this very important spiritual principle. The world, not knowing God in His power and glory, will always see "important" people as the ultimate point of attention. But it is an absolute tragedy when the Church gets caught in the same trap.

Welcoming the Greatest

The subject of who is great among men always has and always will be a sensitive issue as long as there are men and women on earth with carnal temptations. Remember Jesus' disciples in Mark 9: *"When He was in the house, He asked them, 'What were you arguing about on the road?' But they kept quiet because on the way they had argued about who was the greatest"* (Mark 9:33–34).

Unfortunately, this was not the only time in the history of Christianity that this argument was going on. We repeat, Lucifer knows that this attitude, the one that got him thrown out of heaven, is a very effective way to paralyze Christians. The Church is today filled with a number of unnecessary questions. Who is most popular? Who has the biggest church? Who is the most eloquent speaker? Who authored the best-selling book? Who has the no. 1 song on the charts? Who takes in the biggest offerings? Who looks good on television? Who receives special awards? Who draws the biggest crowds? Even, who wins the most souls? Answer: Who cares?! God certainly doesn't. His Word shows clearly that He is not occupied with popularity contests and attendance records. Granted, the Bible speaks of certain persons who are more well-known than others and certain gatherings that are bigger than others. However, the focus is never placed there. But God is at least concerned about how many souls are won, right?! Absolutely. To the ultimate degree of letting His Son die on a cross for the sake of saving the lost. But not for the purpose of producing statistically magnificent records and thereby elevate certain persons or works above others.

When Jesus asked the disciples about their argument, they kept quiet because they knew it was wrong. They acted like children whose immaturity had taken them into a dead-end street. There simply was no excuse, no explanation, just nothing to say. This is what the Church needs to experience over and over again. A holy quietness, refraining from excuses and explanations which are just silly anyway. In fact, there ought to be a sense of shame over any thought of greatness among men when we stand before an all knowing and all powerful God. In light of His greatness, the attention-on-man syndrome is a sin which must be dealt with through repentance. Jesus then continues by giving His disciples a quick and precise lesson in the workings of God and spiritual maturity. *"If anyone wants to be first, he must be the very last, and the servant of all"* (Mark 9:35).

When Luke recalls the same incident he writes: *"Jesus, knowing their thoughts, took a little child and had him stand beside Him. Then He said to them, 'Whoever welcomes this little child in My name welcomes Me; and whoever welcomes Me welcomes the One who sent Me. For he who is least among you all—he is the greatest'"* (Luke 9:47–48). Note carefully what happens here. Jesus, fully understanding their carnal thoughts, uses an illustration. He puts a child in front of them, the expression of weakness, mild manner, and lack of own strength. But Jesus does not say: "Welcome this little child because he is so mild and weak in himself." No, He says: *"Whoever welcomes this little child in My name welcomes Me."* In other words, the focus should not be on a person's attributes, even if these are spiritually correct, but on Jesus Himself. And of course, Jesus is certainly present with someone who is walking in true dependence on His strength and thus, we do welcome Jesus. *"For he who is the least among you all—he is the greatest."* The "least among us" have denied their own carnal self, drowned in Jesus, and are therefore carrying His greatness wherever they go. These are truly the greatest among us.

So, the question should never be: "Who is doing the best job for God?" It should always be: "What is the Lord doing through whomever?" And when we focus on Jesus' great work, the human instrument becomes incidental. *"Whoever welcomes . . . welcomes Me."* That's where our focus should always be. To look for Jesus in any situation—not the messenger He uses.

The JTB Test

We find a situation in John 3 which, as far as the attitude is concerned has been repeated countless times in the history of the Church. John's disciples came to him and said: *"Rabbi, that man who was with you on the other side of the Jordan—the One you testified about— well, He is baptizing, and everyone is going to Him"* (John 3:26). Competition—a major expression of the attention-on-man syndrome—was there within carnal man from the very introduction of the New Covenant. John's disciples were obviously bothered by the fact that Jesus had bigger crowds now. And remember that they probably did not yet understand who Jesus really was. To them He was just another preacher coming to town who had become more popular among the people. Good old competition! What should they do now with such a popular preacher attracting the big crowds? It might even have an impact in the offering plate! Whenever the attention-on-man syndrome is allowed to prevail, these become big and important issues. However, when we de-mask the infiltration by the enemy through this syndrome, nobody cares anymore. This is exactly what God wants. Who cares who has the biggest crowds and the greatest statistics? The only statistic that counts in God's Kingdom is the Lamb's Book of Life which is outside the control (and inspection!) of any man or human organization anyway.

When we learn to turn away from the focus on man, our weary souls can rest from the notion that there is something going on which we need to defend, preserve and sustain. We do not need to sustain anything for God! We absolutely can't, no matter how hard we try. When we truly understand how

God works, with all energy and power coming from Himself and all glory and attention going to Himself, man's role is put in its proper perspective. We will then stop worrying about issues of competition since man is simply an instrument in the hands of Him who no one can compete with anyway.

John answers this situation as a truly "great" servant of God. "*A man can receive only what is given him from Heaven*" (John 3:26). This must be the view of every true servant of God. I have nothing, I can do nothing, I am nothing in myself. Whatever is being done through someone's life is a result of what has been given from heaven—nothing else. Again we see that the focus is on the Giver and not on the gift or instrument He might use. This is a lesson both for the ones in the pulpit and those in the audience. Anytime God uses someone in a special way on a more visible level than others, which He will continue to do, let's react like this: he/she has nothing, can do nothing, is nothing except for God's hand at work. And if this is in fact true, why then pay so much attention and put such focus on the human instrument? If we learn this lesson, we can truly enjoy and be thankful for those God has chosen to use in His ministry. Their faithful work points us past themselves on to Christ, the Life Giver.

John goes on to testify about Christ and then makes a statement that we would like to call the "John the Baptist" test, (the JTB test): "*He must become greater; I must become less*" (John 3:30). Or, as translated in the King James Bible: "*He must increase, but I must decrease.*" This is a test that any true servant of God must be able to pass. It confronts every fiber in our carnal being. To become less, to decrease in a world where power, glory, and success is the going trend. Be assured that even though John prophesied clearly of Jesus as the Christ, he likely had competitive temptations as well. And it would have been much more comfortable for the flesh in all of us if John instead had been inspired to say: "He must increase—and I must also increase with

Him to become something really big in His Kingdom!" But this is not the way it works in God's domain.

It's true that it's easier to pass the JTB test when you compare yourself to Jesus Christ. After all, who would be so foolish to think that he is greater than Him? But what about the ones Jesus has chosen to use? Remember that John met Jesus as an earthly person and was confronted with the question of competition in the form of flesh and blood. Today we see Jesus and His ministry in the form of His work through other people. We must then also be willing to say: "He must increase—*even through others*—and I must decrease." If John's reasoning is true, that no one can receive anything but that which is given from heaven, what about the gifts that God has given to others who then appear to be "bigger" and "better"? There seems to be a fairly good understanding of the need to give all the glory to God, but not as much willingness to let God achieve His work in any way and through anyone He wants. Let's pray that the glory of God will shine throughout the earth— but let's make sure that it doesn't happen through Brother So-and-So, ministry XYZ or the church down the street! Well, it may not be that drastic, but such tendencies are definitely present within the Church. Yes, we know that we are to give all the glory to God. But often it seems like there is quite a competition going on regarding who will hold the biggest sign saying: "I give all the glory to God!"

The JTB test takes care of all this. When the flesh is crucified in this area, God is free to do His work. The correct attitude is very simple: God, do Your work through whomever, whenever, wherever, You want to do it. Glorify Your name only and no one else's, including mine. The Holy Spirit is the Headmaster who takes us through the JTB test. If we pass the test, He will lead us on to bigger and better things. Yes, *bigger* and *better* because we won't abuse it for our own glory. If we do not pass the test, we will have to take this class over and over again. Sometimes it seems like this is what the Church spends most of its time doing. God has many bigger and better things already prepared for the Church today. We can walk in these good works *"which God prepared in advance for us to do"* only if we have the same attitude as John the Baptist regarding the view of ourselves and others.

Eternal Perspective

When we deal with the question of Man's position in God's work on earth, we must have the eternal perspective. A common misunderstanding, also among Christians, is that we are placed on earth for seventy years or so, to try to reach as high as possible on the scale of human success, hopefully avoiding mediocre performance or complete failure. While it's true that God wants our lives on earth to count for something, we must also understand that immediately following our new birth in Christ, we start to prepare for our eternal position. This preparation is much more important than our earthly concerns. Not the least since we are preparing for all eternity, as opposed to just a small fraction of this timespan called our lifetime on earth. This perspective is important in order for us to understand God's dealings with us in this world. And we will discover that much of what is seen as a plus in the eyes of the world actually ends up on the minus side in God's view and vice versa. In this perspective, we will see a definite correlation between our Christian walk on earth and our position in eternity.

Let's explore two different sides of our Christian life. First: Salvation from sin. Secondly: Service for Christ on earth. These are two sides of our Christian walk that go hand in hand but are also distinctly different. Salvation from sin has nothing to do with our own works, whereas service for Christ definitely involves our works. The scripture is filled with teachings on how to trust in Christ's finished work alone for our salvation. But it is also filled with instructions how to do the right things—

work the right works—in service for Christ on earth.

Sometimes we confuse the two. Many people think that in order to be saved they need to do the right things and be good enough for God through their own works. Others maintain that it's all by grace, so let's get saved, sit back and relax while the Holy Spirit, the angels, and overzealous Christians take care of the work that needs to be done through the Church.

Let's look a little closer at these two sides. Salvation from sin is God's free gift and can be received by faith alone. When mankind stands before God one day to determine where each individual is going to spend eternity, only one question will be important: "Did I believe in Christ and did I trust in His saving work?" The love of God displayed through the blood of Jesus is the only atonement for our sin. That's where new life starts and not by any of our doing.

It is different however, with our service for God on earth. Immediately after we have received new life by faith in Christ, God begins an attempt to use us for His purposes during our life-time. We can either willingly cooperate or refuse to participate. This is where "our" works come in. Many have received the free gift of salvation but carry it only as a ticket of entry in their back pocket to be pulled out when they stand at heaven's gate some day. Yes, they will be saved for eternity but are basically of little value for the Kingdom of God on earth. They have received God's grace and power for salvation, but in a sense rejected His grace and power for service while in the world.

The Apostle Paul talks about Christ as the only foundation to build on, and makes an important statement: *"If any man builds on this foundation using gold, silver, costly stones, wood, hay, or straw, his work will be shown for what it is, because the Day will bring it to light. It will be revealed with fire, and the fire will test the quality of each man's work. If what he has built survives, he will receive his reward. If it is burned up, he will suffer loss; he himself will be saved, but only as one escaping through the flames"*

(1 Cor. 3:12–15). We have the opportunity on earth to build on the Christ foundation with gold, silver, and precious stones. These materials represent solid spiritual values and will stand the fire. But we are also constantly tempted to use wood, hay, and straw instead which represent carnal, worldly behavior and will burn quickly. In fact, these are the only materials left if we do not deliberately choose the materials of solid spiritual quality. As we enter heaven one day, by faith in Jesus only, we will have to face this test of "our" work. The fire will either bring us a reward or provide a "barely making it" experience as described in this Scripture. It is obvious that there will be Christians entering as citizens of heaven who will have nothing of their life's work pass the fire test which could be presented to God for a reward.

The Apostle Paul also teaches certain things in 2 Corinthians which all Christians should pay great attention to. He has just discussed the issue of living on earth (in the body) versus reaching a believer's final goal, heaven. He then makes a very important statement: *"So we make it our goal to please Him, whether we are at home in the body or away from it. For we must all appear before the judgment seat of Christ, that each one may receive what is due him for the things done while in the body, whether good or bad "* (2 Cor. 5:9–10). This occasion, labeled the judgment seat of Christ, is the graduation point between our service for Christ on earth and our reign with Him in eternity. There we will receive the scorecard of our performance on earth. This is the same occasion as *"the Day"* which we have just discussed. A time of total honesty when each Christian will stand before the Lord and receive a complete evaluation of his life's work from Christ's perspective. This passage is slightly different in the King James version: *". . . that everyone may receive the things done in his body, according to that he hath done, whether it be good or bad."* It is as if our life's work is going to be played back to us instantly. This time it is not Christ's work, faithfulness and obedience that is to be scrutinized, which is the case when it is determined who will be allowed to enter heaven. Remember, we can enter into God's presence because He looks at us through the perfect work of Jesus. But at the judgment seat of Christ it is our work, our faithfulness, and obedience which is to be evaluated. Our value system in life will change completely if we understand the reality of this remarkable occasion.

This truth is also strongly emphasized in Revelation. *"Then I heard a voice from heaven say, 'Write: Blessed are the dead who die in the Lord from now on.' 'Yes,' says the Spirit, 'they will rest from their labor, for their deeds will follow them'"* (Rev. 14:13). This scripture is often quoted regarding Christians who have gone to be with the Lord, as we think of their good deeds on earth and thank God for their faithfulness. However, it is important to understand that all our deeds will follow us, good and bad, and will have to pass through the fire-test.

In addition to the judgment seat of Christ, the Apostle Paul also speaks about God's judgment seat. *"For we will all stand before God's judgment seat. It is written: 'As surely as I live', says the Lord, 'every knee will bow before Me; every tongue will confess to God'"* (Rom. 14:10–11). While some hold to the view that God's judgment seat and the judgment seat of Christ are one and the same, it also appears that these may be two different occasions. Here in Romans, Paul talks about every knee bowing and every tongue confessing which is about the same phrase he uses in a well-known passage in Phil. 2. In both these instances he is quoting from the prophet Isaiah. *"Before Me every knee will bow; by Me every tongue will swear. They will say of Me, 'In the Lord alone are righteousness and strength.' All who have raged against Him will come to Him and be put to shame. But in the Lord all the descendants of Israel will be found righteous and will exult"* (Isa. 45:23–25). It appears that God's judgment seat could be the occasion when every human will stand before Him and basically be sentenced to heaven or hell. *"All who have raged against Him will . . . be put to shame. But in the Lord all the descendants of Israel will be found righteous . . ."* The judgment seat of Christ, on the other hand, is for those who've entered heaven by grace and now will have their lives' work tested.

This is the occasion, the judgment seat of Christ, we Christians should have in mind in everything we do. Much more so than our human performance evaluations, popularity contests, awards, Who's Who listings, special recognitions, etc. None of this counts at the judgment seat of Christ. A completely different set of values apply, which is what the Holy Spirit tries to teach us during our whole lifetime. With this day in mind, Paul says that our main goal in life should be *"to please Him."* Not to please ourselves, other Christians, Christian leadership, denominations, our local church, etc., with our Christian activities—simply Him. This is where many believers go wrong. They spend their whole life worrying about their reputation and appearance as viewed by other people, not first the Lord. As a result, all their life's work will be tailored to this attitude. And some Christian leaders are just like politicians in this respect, looking for what the latest "poll" reveals about their popularity among the people. Then we are right back in the attention-on-man syndrome, because we focus on ourselves and others while neglecting to please Him first. It is impossible to truly please the Lord and at the same time hang on to this syndrome. These two attitudes cannot exist together. All this will show up before the judgment seat of Christ where human rewards and recognitions might be little more than firewood.

For example, even good deeds done with a bad motive will cancel out our heavenly reward. Listen to Jesus: *"Be careful not to do your 'acts of righteousness' before men, to be seen by them. If you do, you will have no reward from your Father in heaven"* (Matt. 6:1). The big issue at the judgment seat of Christ will basically be how well we worked to serve, promote, and glorify Christ and Him alone on earth. Or if you will, how much we stepped back so that He could step forward in our lives and do His work through us.

Another interesting aspect of the Day of the Lord is announced through the prophet Isaiah, which would apply to the judgment seat of Christ as well as God's judgment seat. *"The Lord Almighty has a day in store for all the proud and lofty, for all that is exalted (and they will be humbled), for all the cedars of Lebanon, tall and lofty, and all the oaks of Bashan, for all the towering mountains and all the high hills, for every lofty tower and every fortified wall, for every trading ship and every stately vessel. The arrogance of man will be brought low and the pride of man humbled; the Lord alone will be exalted in that day, and the idols will totally disappear.*

Men will flee to caves in the rocks and to holes in the ground from dread of the Lord and the splendor of His majesty, when He rises to shake the earth. In that day men will throw away to rodents and bats their idols of silver and idols of gold, which they made to worship. They will flee to caverns in the rocks and to the overhanging crags from dread of the Lord and the splendor of His majesty when He rises to shake the earth. Stop trusting in man, who has but a breath in his nostrils. Of what account is he?" (Isa. 2:12–22). Great emphasis is given here to the fact that all pride and arrogance among men will be brought low on that day, and the Lord alone will be exalted. Verse 22 is of particular interest, stating that man is only a breath in the bigger scheme of things and should not be trusted in or given undue attention.

Rewards in Heaven

The rewards for "fire-proof" Christians, who will pass the test of the judgment seat of Christ, are basically different "jobs" in the eternal world. We can't earn our salvation but it appears that we can earn different positions in eternity based on our faithfulness and endurance on earth. *"Here is a trustworthy saying: 'If we died with Him, we will also live with Him; if we endure, we will also reign with Him'"* (2 Tim. 2:11–12). The Scripture is very clear that everyone is treated equal regarding salvation from sin, but not everyone will have the same position in the eternal world. Our life for Christ on earth basically becomes a résumé for job applications in eternity. A life filled with true spiritual values earns a better job. It's as simple as that. It should be clearly understood however, that these "special position" rewards will be received and held completely without competition, boasting, or jealousy, as we know it here on earth. Such carnal expressions will not be part of the heavenly Kingdom. These rewards are to be used only to serve and glorify the Lord further. Not as trophies in front of each other.

We find a situation in Matthew 20 which illustrates the different positions in the heavenly Kingdom, as well as typical human behavior on earth. *"Then the mother of Zebedee's sons came to Jesus with her sons and, kneeling down, asked a favor of Him. 'What is it you want?' He asked. She said, 'Grant that one of these two sons of mine may sit at Your right and the other at Your left in Your Kingdom.' 'You don't know what you are asking,' Jesus said to them. 'Can you drink the cup I am going to drink?' 'We can,' they answered. Jesus said to them, 'You will indeed drink from My cup, but to sit at My right or at My left is not for Me to grant. These places belong to those for whom they have been prepared by My Father'"* (Matt. 20:20–23). Again, this is a typical situation where people sought after prestigious positions within the Kingdom. Jesus, revealing their lack of understanding in this area, (i.e. *"You don't know what you are asking"*), immediately instructs them that it works differently from Kingdom perspective. The Father alone grants positions according to His value system. This system is completely different from that of the world. We are not to seek power, position and prestige for ourselves or encourage this in each other. If we do, we have failed in the eyes of God. The Lord is trying, over and over again, to teach us the correct order of priority. The first will be the last and the last will be the first.

It is also quite interesting to study the messages which Jesus gives to the seven churches through the Apostle John in Revelation. John saw Jesus in His glorified state, probably much like the way we will see Him at the judgment seat of Christ. "*I turned around to see the voice that was speaking to me. And when I turned I saw seven golden lampstands, and among the lampstands was someone 'like a son of man,' dressed in a robe reaching down to His feet and with a golden sash around His chest. His head and hair were white like wool, as white as snow, and His eyes were like blazing fire. His feet were like bronze glowing in a furnace, and His voice was like the sound of rushing waters. In His right hand He held seven stars, and out of His mouth came a sharp double-edged sword. His face was like the sun shining in all its brilliance*" (Rev. 1:12–16). Jesus then instructs John to write seven specific messages to seven churches. These were words of positive encouragement as well as words of harsh rebuke regarding wrongful behavior. The Lord always speaks the truth, and so should we. There is a constant danger in the Church to try to take a "positive" approach and not deal with that which actually is very serious in the eyes of God. To correctly discern and address the "negative" aspects of the life of the Church is very important. These letters from Jesus are strong proof of that.

Let's look at a particular statement made here by the Lord in light of our study concerning the eternal perspective and rewards in heaven. In each of these letters, found in Revelation chapter 2 and 3, Jesus makes the same statement: "*He who overcomes . . .*" or "*to him who overcomes . . .*" Following this statement are different promises in different letters such as: he will have the right to eat from the tree of life; will not be hurt by the second death; will receive the hidden manna; will be a pillar in God's temple; will have the right to sit with Jesus on His throne; is assured that his name will never be erased from the book of life, etc. All these promises appear to have to do with the glory of reaching heaven by God's grace and be able to enjoy the benefits of such an existence, i.e., the rights and privileges of any citizen of Heaven. However, in His message to the church in Thyatira, Jesus expands on His statement regarding overcomers, indicating that some will have a different role in the heavenly Kingdom. "*To him who overcomes*

and does My will to the end, *I will give authority over the nations—
he will rule them with an iron scepter; he will dash them to pieces
like pottery—just as I have received authority from My Father. I
will also give him the morning star"* (Rev. 2:26–28, bolded by
author).

The statement used in the messages to all the churches, *"Him
who overcomes,"* is directly related to the finished work of Jesus
on the cross. *"They overcame him* (Satan) *by the blood of the Lamb
and by the word of their testimony"* (Rev. 12:11). We become
citizens of heaven by the blood of Jesus and our confession of
faith in His finished work. Any person entering heaven will do it
as an overcomer based on this fact alone. To overcome sin and
gain access to heaven has nothing to do with our work, only the
work of Christ. But the additional statement in the Thyatira letter, *". . . and does My will to the end . . .", (". . . and keepeth My
works unto the end . . ."* King James), adds another dimension of
special authority and position for man in the heavenly Kingdom.
*"To him . . . I will give authority over the nations . . . just as I have
received authority from My Father."* It appears that this is directly
related to God's reward system. We can overcome only by the blood
of the Lamb. But to do His will and His works unto the end—
while still only possible through the power of the Spirit—yet it
requires additional action and effort on our part. And this kind of
faithful service on earth appears to be rewarded in a special way in
heaven. This is why Jesus promises not only the "general" benefits
of heavenly citizenship but special position and authority to this
category.

In addition, Jesus states: *"I will also give him the morning star."*
This is the title used in Isaiah 14 which, as discussed earlier, many
believe to be an account of Satan's fall as he was cast down from
his angelic position. *"How you have fallen from heaven, O morning star . . . !"* As a result, Satan instead became known under
other names, such as destroyer, dragon, serpent, god of this age,
etc. When Jesus finishes the Revelation to John, He uses this title

for Himself. *"I am the Root and the Offspring of David, and the bright Morning Star."* (Rev. 22:16) Jesus has now completely defeated Satan and taken possession of all authority and glory. And when addressing the seven churches, He appears to indicate that this *"morning star"* glory will be given to faithful overcomers. This is a remarkable progression of heavenly power and glory in eternal history.

It is interesting to note how strongly Jesus establishes the kind of authority this will entail. *"To him . . . I will give authority over the nations. He will rule them with an iron scepter; he will dash them to pieces like pottery."* This is a direct quote from Psalm 2:9, a prophecy about Jesus Himself and the authority which was to be given to Him by the Father because of the cross. Jesus now indicates in this eternal perspective that the same authority will be passed along to those who are doing His will to the end. Great authority and special positions are reserved for the "working" and "effective" overcomers.

This fact was also announced earlier as Jesus spoke with His disciples. *"Peter answered Him, 'We have left everything to follow you! What then will there be for us?' Jesus said to them, 'I tell you the truth, at the renewal of all things, when the Son of Man sits on His glorious throne, you who have followed Me will also sit on twelve thrones, judging the twelve tribes of Israel. And everyone who has left houses or brothers or sisters or father or mother or fields for My sake will receive a hundred times as much and will inherit eternal life. But many who are first will be last, and many who are last will be first'"* (Matt. 19:27–30).

Again, Jesus establishes that unselfish and faithful service on earth insures special position in heaven. Not every Christian has left everything to follow Christ, even though they may be believers in His work for their eternal salvation. Not every Christian has given up houses, brothers, fields, etc., for the sake of the Lord. Frankly, some see their relationship to God in the exact opposite light—as an opportunity to gain as much as possible of the above. Not every

Christian has renounced the attitude and system of this world in order to fully comprehend and follow the will of the Lord. Thus, they will be saved, some as through fire, but the positions of authority and prominence in heaven are reserved for those who do. And again, Jesus is here announcing what is bound to be a surprise for all of us in the eternal world. *"But many who are first will be last, and many who are last will be first."* Many who appear to be in high positions of authority on earth had not earned it in the eternal perspective, whereas many who were never seen or applauded on earth will take the real choice spots in the heavenly Kingdom.

Why does God maintain this reverse order in His Kingdom? How can it be that many of those who were the "big" ones on earth may not get the "big" positions in heaven? It has to do with God's value system. In the world: Promote yourself! In the Kingdom of God: Deny yourself! In the world: Glorify yourself! In the Kingdom of God: Glorify Christ only! In the world: Go for the highest and best position! In the Kingdom of God: Seek the lowest position in servanthood! In the world: Get attention and be recognized! In the Kingdom of God: Decrease so that Christ may be seen! In the world: Seek power and control! In the Kingdom of God: Lose all that in Christ! In the world: Exalt yourself for everyone to see! In the Kingdom of God: Humble yourself in the sight of the Lord! And we could go on and on.

Our attitude and actions on earth are carefully being entered into God's "super computer" and will be called up and compared to His value system before the judgment seat of Christ. And, as we have discussed, much of what is counted on the plus-side from the world's perspective, ends up on the minus-side in His system.

Jesus looks at this from a different angle in one of His parables. *"When He noticed how the guests picked the places of honor at the table, He told them this parable: 'When someone invites you to a wedding feast, do not take the place of honor, for a person more distinguished than you may have been invited. If so, the host that invited both of you will come and say to you, "Give this man your* seat." Then, humiliated, you will have to take the least important place. But when you are invited, take the lowest place, so that when your host comes, he will say to you, "Friend, move up to a better place." Then you will be honored in the presence of all your fellow guests. For everyone who exalts himself will be humbled, and he who humbles himself will be exalted'" (Luke 14:7–11).

This parable again deals with God's order of exaltation and humility. Many within the Church try to take up-front positions and exalt themselves. Many are also highly focused on those who seem to have up-front positions in the Christian community. But the Lamb's wedding feast in the eternal world will likely produce some great surprises as to who is going to move up and who is going to move down in the heavenly Kingdom. The lesson is basically this. Do not promote yourself. Then you will be asked to take a lower seat at the table where it really counts — in the eternal world. And, from another perspective, we shouldn't be too enamored with those who presently appear to have up-front positions here on earth. Their seats at God's table might be a lot further down than we think, and we would only look silly having spent so much time and energy focusing on them.

To be in service for God on earth is serious business. We either do it His way and get His job done, or we are in essence useless for His purposes in the world. We repeat again: Our salvation can only be earned by faith in Jesus Christ and that alone. But our willingness to turn away from the attitude of this world and serve God on earth according to His value system will determine our eternal reward. "For the Son of Man is going to come in His Father's glory with His angels, and then He will reward each person according to what he has done" (Matt. 16:27). If we receive understanding of God's eternal perspective — the only one that counts — we will start to re-evaluate many things pertaining to man's position in the work of God. We will see the attention-on-man syndrome — be it attention on ourselves or others — as something of wood, hay, and straw that must be dealt with. This syndrome cannot live side by side with humility and meekness. We must therefore turn away from this carnal attitude and choose the mind of Christ.

ᘒ Chapter 3 ᘒ
IDOLATRY

The One and Only God

God has made it very clear that He does not accept anything or anyone that competes with His supreme position in any way, shape, or form. The first Commandment spells it out: *"You shall have no other gods before Me"* (Exod. 20:3). God knows better than anyone else that there are no other gods but Himself. So why then would He instruct men to not pursue other gods if there aren't any? Simply because He knows that man could very easily begin to worship other things which then in essence would compete with Him as the One and only God. *"Do not make any gods to be alongside Me; do not make for yourselves gods of silver or gods of gold"* (Exod. 20:23). God spoke this through Moses after having put on a show of thunder and lightning, sound and smoke, as if to really underscore the point.

The area of idolatry, to worship anything alongside or instead of Him, is very sensitive with God. *"Be careful to do everything I have said to you. Do not invoke the names of other gods; do not let them be heard on your lips"* (Exod. 23:13). Again, there truly are no other gods, yet the Almighty constantly warns His people to not even come close to pursuing anything in that direction. In fact, He has extremely strong feelings in this area. *"You shall not make for yourself an idol in the form of anything in heaven above or on earth beneath or in the waters below. You shall not bow down to them or worship them; for I, the Lord your God, am a jealous God "* (Exod. 20:4–5). *"Do not worship any other god, for the Lord, whose name is Jealous, is a jealous God "* (Exod. 34:14). These strong feelings within God are the same as can exist within a marriage. Indeed, the Lord is the husband of His people and is therefore jealous for the total love and attention in that union. His Spirit within us constantly yearns for that position. *"You [are like] unfaithful wives [having illicit love affairs with the world and breaking your marriage vow to God]! Do you not know that being the world's friend is being God's enemy? So whoever chooses to be a friend of the world takes his stand as an enemy of God. Or do you suppose that the Scripture is speaking to no purpose that says, The Spirit whom He has caused to dwell in us yearns over us and He yearns for the Spirit [to be welcome] with a jealous love?"* (Jas. 4:4–5 Ampl.).

Jealousy is a carnal attitude which is part of our old nature and should not be tolerated *except* within marriage. If two parties have vowed to belong to each other to the extent that happens in marriage and one of the parties starts to show interest elsewhere, jealousy is an acceptable reaction. As we have already seen, this is exactly what happens even with God Himself. He will not allow anything to compete with our love and attention for Him, or He will become jealous. This is essentially what idolatry is all about. Thus, we must love Him more than anything else—even above family bonds on earth. *"Anyone who loves his father or mother more than Me is not worthy of Me; anyone who loves his son or daughter more than Me is not worthy of Me"* (Matt. 10:37). We must totally focus on the God of the Trinity; Father, Son and Holy Spirit, and on Him alone. *"I am the Lord; that is My name! I will not give My glory to another or My praise to idols"* (Isa. 42:8). Anything else is or borderlines on idolatry and makes it impossible for the Church to move forward in power.

Generally speaking, there are various forms of idolatry. There is the worship of stones, trees, etc., often carved into images of gods. There is also the worship of the sun, moon, and forces of nature. Another area is the worship of heroes, where man takes a special position. The Bible also speaks of less obvious forms of idolatry, such as greed. *"Put to death therefore, whatever belongs to your earthly nature: sexual immorality, impurity, lust, evil desires and greed which is idolatry. Because of these, the wrath of God is coming"* (Col. 3:5–6). In this study however, we will concentrate on the area of hero worship as it relates to the attention-on-man syndrome within the Church.

Modern Religiosity

It is becoming less common in our days to worship statues or the sun and moon as gods in themselves. Modern man is less likely to dance around figures of imaginary handiwork. But he is just as idolatrous as ever, only in a different way. Modern religions, such as secular humanism, the New Age movement, etc., are the carriers of a new breed of "gods." The common denominator for many of these religious movements is that there is no personal God, but that "god" is merely the sum of many forces in the universe. Man has the source of truth and right within himself, and has unlimited powers within his own mind which need only to be unlocked. These movements encompass many concepts from Christianity such as love, forgiveness, tolerance, etc., while leaving out others such as sin and the saving work of Christ. In essence, man is his own god and the work of Christ isn't needed. Man has the ability within himself to reason and can therefore solve his own problems just by unlocking these abilities. This will then supposedly lead to a world of peace, love, and understanding. It appeals very much to modern man who thinks that this approach is quite logical rather than looking for an external God somewhere out there.

In these movements, even though there may not be carved images to bow down to, there is a blatant violation of God's commandment: *"You shall have no other gods before Me."* Man sets himself up as a replacement source for the only true God and looks to his own system and understanding for that which can only be provided by God Himself. Creation becomes the source—not the Creator. Love becomes the source—not the Giver of love. Human reason becomes the source—not the One who is the very origin of wisdom. This is idolatry just as much as praying to a stone image.

And here is the important lesson in light of the attention-on-man syndrome in the Church. These movements, with their faceless, abstract gods, are relying totally on the abilities of men and women to articulate the ideas to others by emotional and intellectual means. Even though they are not actually called "gods," the world is full of "enlightened" men and women who relentlessly teach these idolatrous doctrines. As Christians we know that Satan is behind all this. But the role of man in these movements is essential. Man touches man and the movement spreads. The "teacher's" understanding sets the student "free," and he in turn can touch others.

This is where the Church must watch out with regards to its own leadership. It is not the understanding of the messenger that sets us free. It is the power of God through Jesus Christ, because *"If the Son sets you free, you will be free indeed "* (John 8:36). It is not the Bible teacher's ability to decipher hard-to-understand scripture passages that touches us. It is the Spirit of God, *"for the letter kills, but the Spirit gives life"* (2 Cor. 3:6). It is not the enthusiasm and energy of a fired-up preacher which turns our sorrow into joy. It is Christ Himself who prayed, *"that they may have the full measure of My joy within them"* (John 17:13). It is not the beautiful voices of Christian singers, backed by high-powered synthesizers, that put music in our lives. It is the Lord who *"put a new song in my mouth, a hymn of praise to our God "* (Ps. 40:3).

So, if we within the Church put undue attention on man's ability and strength—even the ability to communicate the Word of God—we will border on idolatry. The messenger can easily become an idol, if we wrongfully focus on his/her ability to communicate the ways of God. We must clearly understand that it is not the channel carrying the light that is important but rather the Light Himself. Remember what was said about John the Baptist: *"He himself was not the light; he came only as a witness to the light. The true light that gives light to every man was coming into the world "* (John 1:8–9). If man is not the light, he is not supposed to shine either as far as his own abilities are concerned. This is a simple but important lesson for the Church.

Hero Worship

Hero worship has always been common among man. People with special abilities have always been admired. History is basically shaped by heroes, men and women elevated above others as leaders, taking people in different directions. Hero worship has led mankind into many unfortunate situations such as what happened under Hitler in Germany. To the old Greeks, a hero was one who lived and died as a mortal being but still was rendered immortal by his ability, character, etc. The Greeks used burial grounds of heroes as places of worship. Today, our heroes are politicians, business magnates, athletes, musicians, movie stars, etc., who influence and lead people.

In modern times, heroes have become less subject to cult worship in the style of the ancient days, although that still happens sometimes. They are now simply called VIPs or celebrities. Still, many of the notions and usages associated with our ancient predecessors survive in different forms. Buildings and mausoleums may be erected in their name. Their homes might become shrines for tourists, just like places of heroes often did in the ancient days. Sometimes their death/birthdays are marked by commemorative exercises. Instead of old time minstrels reciting the greatness of ancient heroes, celebrities now have managers and publicity agents. Instead of cultic following, they might now have fan clubs and mailing lists. Their charisma is no longer enlisted to promote fertility and good crops, but might instead be used for endorsements of products and ideas.

Heroes, particularly of the stage, are often called "stars" which is now also frequently used in Christian circles. This seemingly innocent definition of somebody with celebrity status is a direct derivative from ancient astrology. The ancient Greeks and Romans have tales where heroes, as rewards for extraordinary feats, actually became stars in the sky. This way of thinking is likely what the Apostle Paul refers to in Philippians: "... *children of God without fault in a crooked and depraved generation, in which you shine like stars in the universe as you hold out the word of life* ..." (Phil. 2:15–16). Not that Paul would suggest that there are special "stars" among Christians, but that every Christian is a "star" because of the shining light of Jesus in him. Another word for stars today is actually "idols," which symbolizes people who have reached a certain level of admiration from others. All this comes awfully close to ancient idolatry. In fact, the focus on stars and idols is still a major source of enjoyment and what seems to be fulfillment of life for people worldwide.

The Church must watch itself carefully in this area. There are no true heroes except one—Jesus Christ. It really doesn't matter who does what in the Church, since all of it is the work of the Lord anyway. The messenger is not significant and should not be looked upon as something special, only in the sense that every Christian is special in the eyes of God. Yes, a human being can be a model for others as to how one should follow Christ. But he is not to be focused on—only Christ. Any other attention-on-man attitude will border on idolatry, if not be idolatry itself.

Yes, there is supposed to be great praise in the Kingdom of God—for Him alone who was slain—nobody else. Yes, there is immortality in the Kingdom of God— for everyone who has received Jesus Christ—not just a few special ones. Yes, there is great glory within the Church—the glory of lifting up Jesus only who then will draw all men unto Himself. Any other attitude of attention on man is an abomination in the sight of the Lord. The Church simply must learn to take its eyes off the messengers—the "bad" ones *and* the "good" ones! God is a jealous God and does not share His glory with anyone. Not even His "best" servants!

Media Influence

The continuous development of media technology has great influence on hero worship. Besides printed material, which has been in existence for several hundred years, we are now surrounded by satellites, radio, television, film, telephone, fax machines, records, cassettes, compact discs, video tapes, computers and who knows what else to come. Television in particular has become probably the most influential force throughout the world. Its ability to bring sight and sound around the globe with instant reports of different events has forever changed the makeup of our planet. Television has made it easier than ever to create heroes and celebrities, and to push these to heights never before imagined. In fact, television is a perfect fit for the attention-on-man syndrome and exists largely because of this syndrome.

The largest viewership happens when stars of movies, sitcoms, talk shows, sports, politics, and news appear. This is what makes television thrive. TV producers know this, and are using this technology as a closeup media, i.e., filling the screen frequently with closeups of preferably great celebrities and stars. And these need not be celebrities only because of their ability to do something good and positive. Many have become well-known because of bad and evil things in their lives. Television today does not distinguish between the two, but is only looking for attention (ratings) from the viewership for whatever reason—good or bad. This has an extremely eroding effect on biblical and moral values and is used to the hilt by Satan. Television has today become his best weapon to drive mankind further away from God and to attack those who do believe in biblical values.

The Church must be involved with this media in a new and different way. It cannot hand over this effective tool to the enemy alone. However, only if we receive wisdom from the Spirit to stay away from the attention-on-man syndrome can we effectively use this instrument. If not, it will be a two-edged sword that will cut the wrong way and really hurt us instead. It is difficult to take the focus off man while producing television. The movements of the Holy Spirit cannot be picked up by picture tubes and color correctors. There are no video clips or still frames of Christ in His work on earth which can be used for closeups on the screen. And even if it was possible to catch a glimpse of Jesus in His present, glorified state, it would be quite unhealthy for the equipment! When John saw Jesus in the Revelation at Patmos, he states: *"His face was like the sun shining in all its brilliance"* (Rev. 1:16). Such light intensity would likely be hard on any television facility. Thus, man is primarily the object in front of the camera. In spite of this, the Holy Spirit has a way for us to effectively use this media for the proclamation of the Kingdom of God through our Lord Jesus Christ. But we repeat again, only if we stay clear from the attention-on-man syndrome—whether it is undue attention on ourselves or on others—will this be possible.

As far as man's role is concerned, we must be prepared for such strange concepts (in the eyes of the world) as anti-PR as opposed to "normal" PR; de-promotion as opposed to "normal" promotion; play down publicity as opposed to play it up; actively work to decrease as opposed to increase popularity, etc. This is to ensure that man does not take center stage. We must learn to accept God's strength in our weakness and the fact that He also in the use of modern technology follows His normal pattern: ". . . *God chose the foolish things to shame the wise; God chose the weak things of the world to shame the strong*" (1 Cor. 1:27). This does not mean that we should not aim for high standards of quality. But we are not to adapt the "wisdom" of the world as far as focus on man is concerned if we want to do it God's way. We must learn to accept the strategy and timing of the Lord rather than taking our cues from the world's PR and entertainment machinery.

Remember Jesus at the Feast of Tabernacles. *"But when the Jewish Feast of Tabernacles was near, Jesus' brothers came to Him, 'You ought to leave here and go to Judea, so that Your disciples may see the miracles You do. No one who wants to become a public figure acts in secret. Since You are doing these things, show Yourself to the world'"* (John 7:2–4). This is a situation where the people around Jesus see a publicity opportunity according to the thinking of the world. The same kind of expression is found here which is used for television or any other type of modern day media platform: Show yourself to the world! But Jesus, not moved by hunger for publicity, answers: *"the right time for Me has not yet come; for you any time is right"* (John 7:6). There is a time and a way which is right from a worldly point of view, but not necessarily so from God's perspective. In our days, publicity, advertising, television coverage and the like works according to certain rules. If these rules are followed correctly, they lead to success in attempts to reach and influence the masses. In this situation, Jesus' brothers saw a great PR opportunity for Him based on a going trend. It is very easy to fall into this line of thinking and neglect to consider the number one factor: God's strategy and timing. Jesus was not moved by worldly publicity standards but solely by the hand of the Father working in His life. He did not see the Feast of Tabernacles as a publicity opportunity which absolutely had to be used. Rather, He saw it as yet another situation to serve the Father in doing something or *not* doing something—whichever way the Father would lead Him.

Interestingly, Jesus did go up to the Feast. First in secret and later teaching openly. Not because some PR agents said so, but because the Father led Him. He also delivered one of His "classic" sermons there. *"On the last and greatest day of the Feast, Jesus stood and said in a loud voice, 'If a man is thirsty, let him come to Me and drink. Whoever believes in Me, as the Scripture has said, streams of living water will flow from within him'"* (John 7:37–38). Note that Jesus used all the tools that would have been suggested by PR agents. He spoke this word on the last and greatest day of the Feast when likely the largest number of people were there. This would be the equivalent of using mass media in our days. The Scripture also says that Jesus spoke in a loud voice, likely to be heard by as many as possible—the equivalent of today's sound systems, television cameras and other electronic equipment to effectively communicate the message. Publicity agents would have been proud of Him! However, Jesus did not do this because PR people and media experts said so, but because the Father directed Him this way. There is a world of difference between these two foundations. The outward appearance might look just about the same. But the reason why is drastically different and will actually determine whether there will be *"streams of living water"* involved or not.

The Church must learn to use modern media God's way and not get caught in the attitude of the world while using powerful tools like television. Jesus said: *"But I, when I am lifted up from the earth, will draw all men to Myself"* (John 12:32). To proclaim Jesus' finished work on the cross is the main mission of the Church. The Church cannot draw anyone to the Lord by itself. It has to be done by Christ through the Holy Spirit. But God's people must continually display Jesus as Savior and Lord in order for the Spirit to apply this "magnetic" power to the message. It is therefore extremely important not to lift up any-one else—as is done when focus is placed on man—so that this power-field not be disturbed.

This is a time when the world more and more effectively applies the attention-on-man syndrome through media tech-nologies. The Church must stand doubly strong against this tide. It must be filled with godly revelation and enlightenment when using powerful mass media tools so as to not give the enemy an opportunity for infiltration. The result of such infil-tration can become so much more severe if amplified through modern technologies.

Servants Are Not Nameless or Faceless

We are not trying to say in this teaching that man has to be completely hidden in order for God to use him. It should be clearly understood that God is not doing His work through nameless or faceless people. He uses real-world men and women with real names and real faces. Not mechanical robots without personali-ties or individual style. All throughout the history of Christendom, God has called and used human beings and allowed their lives and service to become an inspiration for others. The Bible even urges us to become models for others and to look up to those who are good models. The Apostle Paul's instructions to Timothy are quite clear: "... *set an example for the believers in speech, in life, in love, in faith and in purity*" (1 Tim. 4:12). In fact, God has even allowed most of the books of the Bible to be clearly identified with the names of the individuals who were inspired by the Spirit to write them. It has always been God's method of operation to call men and women to specific service in His work and allow them to be identified with these specific works. Man will certainly be in the picture of God's work on earth, since the Lord has chosen him as His tool. But the big question is simply this: Where is the focus and main attention? On Him who initiates, performs, and sustains His work, or on the instrument He uses to do so?

Many are familiar with the following technique used in film-making. If two objects are in the picture, one up close and one farther away, the cameraman, by changing the focus on his camera lens, can shift the attention of the viewer between these two objects. He might first focus on the up-front object which will get the attention of the viewer. He then adjusts the focus to concentrate on the object farther away and as a result the attention will shift there instead. The human eye (and mind) tends to always place the attention where the focus is. With this method a filmmaker can make sure that he gets the storyline over to the viewer by focusing the attention in the right direction.

This illustrates well what we are trying to say in our teaching. Christ is always up-front in the picture of all God's work. Everything is done by Him, through Him, and for His glory. Man will also be in the picture simply because God has chosen to use him as His instrument. But again, the important question is: Where is the focus? On Christ or on man? Well, how about focus on both? It doesn't work that way. Focus on one will automatically result in lack of focus on the other, just like in the above film technique. The attention-on-man syndrome has only one setting on its camera lens. Full focus on man! That's why this syndrome is so destructive because it immediately blurs Christ. There is no acceptable compromise. It's one or the other.

Although man is not nameless or faceless in the work of the Lord, it is quite clear that the focus in the Bible is never on man himself—only on God's work through man. The Scripture is not written as a tabloid magazine or a Who's Who listing, highlighting great achievements by famous people or the latest gossip about them. The Bible is a reflection of God's perfect plan worked out among mankind, featuring Jesus as the only celebrity. Contrary to what we often think, the New Testament is not a complete history book on the workings of the early Church. Sometimes we get the idea that every significant event and all the "important" people in the early Church are included. This is not the case. God picked certain events and certain individuals to be included in the Bible for His own reasons. These reasons would include instructions for future believers, etc. But other events and other people — maybe even more "prominent" and seemingly more "significant" at the time — were not included. They have instead been saved for God's eternal history book. The Lord acts according to His specific plan, not according to Man's carnal desire for sensationalism and gossip.

One such example is found in Paul's final greetings in Romans. *"Greet Andronicus and Junias, my relatives who have been in prison with me. They are outstanding among the apostles, and they were in Christ before I was"* (Rom. 16:7). These are two people who apparently were "prominent" in the early Church, but for reasons known only to God, are mentioned just once at the end of one of Paul's letters. There is no "Epistle of Andronicus to the Ephesians" in the Bible, although it is entirely possible that he might have written them a letter. And Junias, possibly the wife or sister of Andronicus since this is a feminine name, is not mentioned again either. Had this happened today, she would have been prominently featured on the front cover of just about every Christian magazine. And certainly a sought-after speaker in women's conferences. After all, she was related to the great Apostle Paul, had suffered in prison with him, and was an outstanding minister herself with a longstanding reputation. This background would just about ensure high visibility in today's Christian world.

Another example is the man who was the object of one of Jesus' most spectacular miracles. John chapter 11 tells us how Lazarus had been dead and buried for several days and had already started to smell of decay when Jesus raised him from the dead. As Jesus loudly called his name: *"Lazarus, come out!"* (John 11:43), he walked out wrapped in his graveclothes. What a view! Just imagine if modern day television cameras had been present. The strong impact that this miracle had on the people was actually what led the Sanhedrin to finally decide to get rid of Jesus. Sometime thereafter, six days before Passover, a dinner was given for Jesus at Bethany where Lazarus also was one of the guests. This is the last we hear of him in Scripture. However, tradition suggests that Lazarus was thirty years old when he died, lived another thirty years after having been brought back to life and, through extraordinary circumstances, came to Cyprus where he became the bishop of the church at Kition. Wouldn't this have been a remarkable story to follow? If you and I had been in charge of the contents of the Bible, we probably wouldn't have missed the opportunity to include the life and work of the church at Kition, whose pastor had been ministered to by Jesus in a way that *very* few could testify about. This would have been an excellent part of the Scripture in our view.

However, God sees things differently. He never acts according to man's PR and publicity schemes based on the attention-on-man syndrome. He only acts according to His perfect plan in order to achieve His eternal purposes. Thus, "significant" events and "prominent" people—as seen from our point of view—may be a lot less important in His view and not given the level of visibility we think they should have. This is a very important understanding as we look at man's role in God's work.

Is God Alone our Source?

The issue of idolatry is really determined by one simple question: Is God alone our source? God reacted severely when His people in the Old Testament turned to something else other than Him as their source. *"'I will hide My face from them,' He said, 'and see what their end will be; for they are a perverse generation, children who are unfaithful. They made Me jealous by what is no god and angered Me with their worthless idols'"* (Deut. 32:20–21). So often the Israelites displayed the attitude that God as their only source was not enough. Shortly after they left captivity, they started to hunger for the meat of Egypt, as if God couldn't feed them. When Moses, in their opinion, tarried a little too long on the mountain, they turned to an idol in the form of a golden calf. At Kadesh Barnea, on the border of the Promised Land, they looked at the giants and thought that they were too big for God. It had to be accomplished in some other way. When finally entering the Promised Land and driving out different peoples before them, they frequently turned to the practice of idolatry among these groups. Sometimes it became a total abandonment of the one and only God. But many times it was simply the feeling that they needed something in addition to Him. It was as if they did not trust God to be their sole source.

This is where the Church must learn an important lesson. The Lord Jesus is the Head of the Body of Christ and the sole Provider through His Holy Spirit. He is our one and only Source. Man's role is only to facilitate His work and return all the glory to Him. Any other attitude borders on idolatry and the attention-on-man syndrome is extremely dangerous in this respect.

We could ask ourselves some simple questions which would reveal our view of the source. Is the Word of God more powerful when Sister Somebody speaks, or is it just as powerful if Brother Nobody does under the same anointing? Is Scripture more effective if Brother Sing-a-Loud communicates with a beautiful voice, or is it just as good if Sister No-Pitch does? Is God's Kingdom more powerful when multiple thousands of Christians have been drawn together with the help of some well-known VIP names, or is it just as effective when two persons are gathered in His name? Am I just as willing and happy to participate in a small "insignificant" gathering as in the big, well produced Christian event with famous speakers and singers? It we cannot firmly and correctly answer these and similar questions — indicating that our spiritual sight is clear — we have thereby proven to ourselves that we have made man a partial source beside God and thus are in great danger of idolatry.

Perhaps we should start taking an entirely different view of the whole issue of being ministered to by others. A common attitude today is to seek out anointed men and women with great "credentials" and high visibility. We attend gatherings where they minister so that we may receive a fresh word from the Lord. While God certainly uses these occasions in His work, maybe it is time to stop "seeking" the messengers in order to seek God alone, so that He may send whatever messenger He wants to us. In other words, instead of you seeking out the messenger, let the messenger seek you out. It should be noted however, that this view is not to be taken as a license for spiritual laziness, skipping church, or shunning personal responsibility to follow God. Rather, to diligently proceed in one's spiritual walk, but with much less emphasis on who the Lord might use to feed us spiritually.

We will find that God sometimes uses the big event, and other times sends a Nobody from Nowhere to accomplish His purposes in our lives. The attention-on-man syndrome, however, creates a big problem in this respect. If we are influenced by this syndrome, we will have a hard time believing that God can use a "nobody" for anything. Thus, we will miss much of God's work, since this is the backbone of His strategy — to use that which is "nothing."

Where does the Church stand in practical reality with respect to its view of the source? Do we see heroes as a necessary ingredient in the life of the Church? Are we maintaining celebrities, VIPs, and stars which reach a certain level of admiration from others, so that we may give God credibility on earth? Are we so conformed to the system of this world that we feel compelled to glorify certain men and women in order to thereby bring visibility to God's

Word? Have we in fact made a modified version of hero worship a partial source of the function of the Church? It does appear many times that we have. This does not help the work of the Church, although it seemingly does so for a season. Instead, it will hinder the long-range plan of God. This does not mean that everyone with a visible position leads others into idolatry. Scripture speaks strongly about true spiritual leadership which we will discuss later. God will always use certain men and women on a more visible level than others in His work. But again, we must clarify our perception of the source.

Ancient idols were all man-made and had nothing to do with the work of God other than the fact that He created the raw material used to make these; wood, stone, etc., in the first place. The perception that certain people are celebrities and stars, using gifts and talents which also come from God in the first place, is man-made as well. Such a perception is as wrong and ineffective in God's eyes as wooden idols. In fact, true spiritual work done through someone on a visible level will be hindered greatly if Christians become focused on the visibility itself and start to see a celebrity rather than a channel for the work and glory of Christ.

Only that which is born by the Spirit within a human being can be used by God for His purposes. Therefore, the focus should always be on the spiritual actions taken by Christ. Not on the style and outward attributes of the instrument He uses for the moment. A true messenger from God will always give Him all the glory and strive to stay in the background so that Christ alone can be clearly seen. Thus, making it easy for others to focus on the Lord. The messenger will be part of the picture but will not take any attention away from Christ. The attention-on-man syndrome on the other hand, is man-made and man-centered, thus an abomination in God's sight just like idol worship.

Remember our statement earlier that the entertainment industry really is a false attempt by Satan to create joy and fulfillment for people while leaving out God. This industry is totally dependent on hero worship. There must be a constant stream of new celebrities and stars in order for the entertainment world to stay alive and vigorous. The Church must absolutely separate itself from this attitude and not fall into the trap which can lead to idolatry. If anything, we should take cues from the secular entertainment industry on how not to do it instead of the other way around.

High Places

Let's explore a significant situation involving King Solomon. *"Solomon showed his love for the Lord by walking according to the statutes of his father David, except that he offered sacrifices and burned incense on the high places"* (1 Kings 3:3). Before King David died he had instructed his son Solomon to walk in the ways of the Lord and obey His commands. Then God would keep His promise to David, that there would always be one of his descendants on the throne of Israel. This promise was ultimately fulfilled in Jesus Christ. Solomon apparently obeyed his father in this respect, except for his attraction to the "high places." Scripture does not say that he worshiped other gods or offered sacrifices to idols (at this point). He worshiped the God of Israel, but sometimes in the wrong way, on the "high places." These "high places" were sites of pagan worship and even though the Israelites conquered these places and used them to worship the Lord, He still was not pleased. It was too close to pagan worship, even though they did not worship pagan gods, for the Lord Almighty to be comfortable.

The attention-on-man syndrome is today the equivalent of such a "high place." We do not intend to worship anyone but God alone and His Son Jesus Christ. But we do it in such a way that we create a "high place" which comes much too close to idolatry in the eyes of God. We adopt a worldly VIP/celebrity system because it seemingly gives high visibility to the work of

God, just like the "high places" of old with altars on hills and mountains to be clearly seen. This appears many times to be a good way of serving God but may in fact have the opposite effect. Remember Jesus' answer to the Samaritan woman when she asked Him about where and how to worship: *"Yet a time is coming and has now come when the true worshipers will worship the Father in spirit and truth, for they are the kind of worshipers the Father seeks. God is spirit, and His worshipers must worship Him in spirit and in truth"* (John 4:23–24).

Worship of God can only be done *"in spirit and in truth"* if it stays away from the flesh. God is spirit and must be worshiped that way. Man's spirit can do one thing only: reach out to God through Jesus Christ with full attention on Him, giving all the glory to Him. If there is any, even a minute percentage, of shared attention and glory, we can be assured that this is not driven by spirit but flesh. Thus, to worship in spirit and truth, we must totally turn away from the attention-on-man syndrome and concentrate on the Lord alone. We cannot use the "high places" to assist God in His attempt to fellowship with man.

Interestingly, God did not turn His back on Solomon immediately just as He hasn't closed down the Church simply because there are things going on among His people which are not pleasing to Him. As a matter of fact, it was when Solomon offered sacrifices to God on one of these high places that God appeared to him and told him to ask for whatever he wanted. God is merciful and shows great patience in calling us to repentance. This doesn't mean, however, that we should relax in our wrongful ways and abuse His mercy. We must constantly seek Him with a repentant heart and be prepared to change our ways as He reveals His Kingdom to us. Solomon asked for wisdom and understanding which was given to him in great measure. He became a great king and built the temple to the Lord which was the dream of his father David. However, the last chapter of his life is a sad one.

"King Solomon, however, loved many foreign women . . . They were from nations about which the Lord had told the Israelites, 'You must not intermarry with them, because they will surely turn your hearts after their gods.' . . . As Solomon grew old, his wives turned his heart after other gods, and his heart was not fully devoted to the Lord his God, as the heart of David his father had been. . . . On a hill east of Jerusalem, Solomon built a high place for Chemosh the detestable god of Moab, and for Molech the detestable god of the Ammonites. . . . The Lord became angry with Solomon because his heart had been turned away from the Lord, the God of Israel . . . . So the Lord said to Solomon, 'Since this is your attitude and you have not kept My covenant and My decrees, which I commanded you, I will most certainly tear the kingdom away from you and give it to one of your subordinates. Nevertheless, for the sake of your father, I will not do it during your lifetime'" (1 Kings 11:1–12).

It's very likely that this tragic ending of a man who had received great wisdom and discernment from God, was due to his flirtation with the high places in the beginning. At first, they seemed to be only a "convenient" tool to effectively serve and worship the One and only true God. But in the end, it turned into full-fledged idolatry in such a way that his kingdom could not be preserved. This is exactly what happens with hero worship within the Church. It seems to be an effective tool to accomplish the work of God, but in the end it has destroyed more than it has built up. God's people must stay away from the "high places" and worship God in spirit and in truth. This is the only way that the Church can truly be a spiritual Kingdom in a time when we are presented with more and more sophisticated versions of the attention-on-man syndrome.

Finances

When we look at the attention-on-man syndrome within the Church, we must mention a very simple, underlying reason for the persistence of this syndrome: Money. Everybody knows that the secular entertainment world keeps a constant string of celebrities and stars going in order to make money. It works a little different in the Christian world, but unfortunately the principle is sometimes the same. The goal for most Christians is not to get rich off the Church, although there are certainly some that have fallen into that trap. But it basically works this way. In order to provide finances for God's work, to keep church and ministry budgets going, to support missionary work, to pay for seminars and conferences, etc., we need strong and popular names in order to keep gifts, offerings, and other forms of financial support flowing. If the pastor is revered and appreciated—the church budget is secured. If a large "ministry" has a well-known and highly visible leader— it is a lot easier to keep things going financially. If a Christian "celebrity" endorses a missions project or charity work—it is more likely to succeed. Most of these works are worthy efforts in the Kingdom of God and should certainly be supported. But the problem is that we are more and more adapting the attention-on-man syndrome in order to do what is supposed to be done as unto the Lord. We seem to be more apt to support people rather than the works they have been called to do. We are not saying that individuals who have gained respect among others because of their special call and faithful service to the Lord, (if that is, in fact, the reason for their notability), should not be able to speak out about certain works within the Church. But there is a danger zone in this area where we—in our eagerness to do what is good and right—are crossing the line to hero worship, thereby destroying the good purpose.

While understanding the need for finances to support the work of God and with due respect for those who have responsibilities in this area, we still need to take a close look at the fundraising and merchandising machinery in the Church today. Let's be honest: The Church is big business! And there is only a fine line between the need to have systems and organizations in place which can truly assist the Church financially, and a self-seeking industry which focuses on gains and profits instead. The area of hero worship becomes even more prevalent when we cross that fine line. If we begin to look at the work of God in a carnal way as a business opportunity, we also begin to accept carnal means to achieve our goals. We repeat again that the entertainment industry is totally dependent on celebrities and stars to keep going. Have we in fact adopted much of the same system within the Church, even when our motives to serve God are largely right and good? In our eagerness to support the work of God—whether on the stage or in the audience—have we wrongfully focused on man and made God subject to the endorsement of man? Is this the way the work of the Lord is supposed to be done?

The area of finances is most sensitive and every Christian—shepherd or sheep—needs to be alert so as to not give the devil a foothold. Scripture speaks strongly about greed, defined as a desire for more than one needs or deserves. If the finance machinery in the Church supports greed in any form, it has thereby proven itself to be idolatrous. We repeat again from Colossians: "*Put to death, therefore, whatever belongs to your earthly nature: sexual immorality, impurity, lust, evil desires and greed, which is idolatry. Because of these, the wrath of God is coming.*" A major tool to satisfy idolatrous greed, even within the Church, is the attention-on-man syndrome around which you can build big business in the same manner as the secular entertainment industry.

On a side-note, wrongful emphasis on prosperity and blessings from God can easily turn into greed and subsequent idolatry. If we focus on God's gifts and provisions—particularly in the material realm—instead of the Giver Himself, we will very easily introduce the greed-factor. We start to worship the gifts rather than the Giver. We might use all the right words and outward gestures as if the Lord is truly the center of our attention. But it's really the gifts and the prosperity we are after. In that case, we can look forward to God's wrath rather than His blessing. Remember, He is greatly bothered by idolatry.

Let's also look at the situation when Paul and Silas ended up in prison in Philippi. *"Once when we were going to the place of prayer, we were met by a slave girl who had a spirit by which she predicted the future. She earned a great deal of money for her owners by fortune telling. This girl followed Paul and the rest of us, shouting, 'These men are servants of the Most High God who are telling you the way to be saved.' She kept this up for many days. Finally, Paul became so troubled that he turned around and said to the spirit, 'In the name of Jesus Christ I command you to come out of her!' At that moment the spirit left her. When the owners of the slave girl realized that their hope of making money was gone, they seized Paul and Silas and dragged them into the marketplace to face the authorities"* (Acts 16:16–19).

Money was the pure and simple issue here. The spirit of divination (fortunetelling) within this slave girl had created a great business opportunity for some people in town. Interestingly, at this particular time the evil spirit had led her to speak the truth that Paul and Silas were servants of God, teaching the way of salvation. Paul discerned that this was all done in the wrong spirit and for the wrong reasons and cast the spirit out of her. The owners of the slave girl could immediately envision declining profits for their business and got so angry that they arranged to have God's servants thrown in jail.

By the way, out of this situation came a great miracle where God shook the prison, opened the doors, and saved the jailer and his household. It is also one of the very few times recorded in the New Testament where music and singing were used in the work of God, as Paul and Silas prayed and sang praise songs in their cell while the other prisoners listened. The first Church most certainly used music in its worship of the Lord. But it is not given a prominent place in the New Testament. Perhaps this is another lesson for the Church today, where we have put such an extreme emphasis on the pleasure of the music itself.

The slave girl in this situation had become a great attraction and the basis for big business. Never mind the spiritual values, positive or negative. Let's just make money! This is certainly the going trend in the world today as well. The Church must be ultra careful in this area. Nothing can corrupt like money. Nothing can make people compromise in their value judgments like money. Nothing, like money, can take good people heading in the right direction and turn them into compromisers, heading in the wrong direction. Scripture states it very clearly: *"For the love of money is the root of all kinds of evil"* (1 Tim. 6:10).

The prophet Hosea defined idolatry as a spirit of prostitution. "A *spirit of prostitution leads them astray; they are unfaithful to their God"* (Hosea 4:12). Prostitution is the act of taking the God-intended, intimate relationship of marriage and turning it into wrongful, adulterous pleasure and profit. Hosea warned the people that idolatry is prostitution because it is unfaithfulness to God. And the spirit of prostitution lives on under the attention-on-man syndrome. This syndrome takes away full attention from the Lord and we continue to "buy" and "sell" ourselves and each other when we have this focus. God has to share the stage with us and we have thereby created a subtle and sophisticated form of unfaithfulness to Him. The spirit of prostitution must be shunned at any cost.

Again, with due respect for those whom God has given stewardship responsibilities over the financial affairs of the Church, we still must not cross over the line between the "meeting the needs" area and the "love of money" territory. It is very easy to miss the mark here. If we feel compelled to introduce a worldly attention-on-man system in order to be financially successful within the Church, we are thereby in danger of creating a double dose of idolatry: Hero worship and greed. We can be most assured that this is not pleasing to God!

∽Chapter 4∾
SPIRITUAL LEADERSHIP

To Build up the Church

The attention-on-man syndrome is particularly damaging in the area of spiritual leadership. If Satan is successful in turning our attention more or less to the instrument God is using rather than to the Lord Himself, he has gained an upper hand in the spiritual battle. Let us look at a few things which are important in order for spiritual leadership to function properly within the Church.

The goal of leadership is to build up and strengthen the Body of Christ. Paul's teaching in Ephesians is well-known: *"It was He who gave some to be apostles, some to be prophets, some to be evangelists, and some to be pastors and teachers, to prepare God's people for works of service, so that the Body of Christ may be built up until we all reach unity in the faith and in the knowledge of the Son of God and become mature, attaining to the whole measure of the fullness of Christ. Then we will no longer be infants, tossed back and forth by the waves, and blown here and there by every wind of teaching and by the cunning and craftiness of men in their deceitful scheming. Instead, speaking the truth in love, we will in all things grow up into Him who is the Head, that is, Christ. From Him the whole Body, joined and held together by every supporting ligament, grows and builds itself up in love, as each part does its work"* (Eph. 4:11–16). Notice the particular role that is given to spiritual leadership in this passage: *". . . to prepare God's people for works of service, so that the Body of Christ may be built up . . ."* Notice also that the goal for the build-up is growth into Christ based on His attitude and authority, not allegiance to the leadership itself. *"Instead . . . we will in all things grow up into Him . . ."* Notice further that leadership itself does not provide the growth. It only facilitates growth which comes from Christ, the Head. *"From Him the whole Body . . . grows and builds itself up . . ."* Christ is the only source of life and growth for the Body. Man, whether in a behind-the-scenes position or on a highly visible level of leadership, can only serve as a channel for Christ's work and power, never be the source himself. All spiritual growth within the Church comes *"from Him."* However, for Christ to accomplish His work in and through the Body it is required that *"each part does its work."* This is where spiritual leadership plays a very important role and our understanding and implementation of such leadership determines the opportunity for the Body to grow.

Let us emphasize again that the goal for spiritual leadership is to build up the Body of Christ. Never itself, or its particular part of the Body. If the focus is put on the leadership itself, it will only deform the Body, not build it up. We have seen many grotesque growths on the Body of Christ because of this attitude, which has greatly diminished its beauty. The attention-on-man syndrome is like a cancer which is only concerned with its own growth with no regard to what this does to the rest of the Body. As we know, cancer is a powerful adverse growth process which, if gone untreated, ultimately leads to death, not life. When the view of leadership—be it by leaders or by those being led—turns to itself, it serves the opposite purpose from what was intended. Instead of building up and uniting, it tears down and divides. Instead of focusing on Christ and His life-giving power, it focuses on man and hinders the flow of life from the Head. It cannot be emphasized strongly enough that spiritual leadership is meant only to focus on and glorify Christ—not itself.

The offices of ministry in Ephesians 4 have sometimes been viewed as positions to be "glorified" in themselves, which are given to "special" people. However, let us ask a simple question: When Paul writes: ". . . *some to be apostles, some to be prophets, some to be evangelists, some to be pastors and teachers . . . ,*" how many are "some"? Is it a certain number for every local church, every city, every country, or worldwide? Or is it one strong man/woman for every area or local church in each of these offices? Or is it what appears to be a random number to the human mind, as God in His divine plan selects certain people for spiritual leadership? Or—on the contrary—is it possible that God in His infinite wisdom has a way to include all believers in the ministry offices which provide leadership to the Church? In other words, some of us are apostles, some are prophets, some are evangelists, etc., but all of us are something in this area. Indeed, when Paul begins this particular teaching, he states: *"But to each one of us grace has been given as Christ apportioned it. This is why it says: 'When He ascended on high, He led captives in His train and gave gifts to men.' . . . It was He who gave some to be apostles, some to be prophets . . ."* (Eph. 4:7–8, 11). This seems to indicate that all Christians, *"each one of us,"* are involved.

Granted, not everyone will lead a large number of people. Most of us will lead only a few, maybe just one person. But the role of a spiritual leader is not defined by the number of "followers," as we often think. It is defined by our obedience to Christ's call, and each leadership position is as important in His eyes whether we will influence one or one thousand. Could it be that this is the true leadership structure of the Church? That we are all leaders as well as followers. After all, every Christian is part of a "*royal priesthood*," not just some priests and others spectators. One expression, used frequently in the Church, really doesn't fit. It is the title "layman" which identifies people of the laity as opposed to the clergy. This expression actually means "not priestly" and is an incorrect label for any Christian. We are all anointed for service through Christ in the New Covenant. Not just certain prophets and priests as in the Old Covenant, whom the people would turn to in order to know God's will.

The Apostle Paul discusses ministry offices/gifts in his first letter to the Corinthians as well. "*Now you are the Body of Christ, and each one of you is a part of it. And in the Church God has appointed first of all apostles, second prophets, third teachers, then workers of miracles, also those having gifts of healing, those able to help others, those with gifts of administration, and those speaking in different kinds of tongues. Are all apostles? Are all prophets? Are all teachers? Do all work miracles? Do all have gifts of healing? Do all speak in tongues? Do all interpret? But eagerly desire the greater gifts*" (1 Cor. 12: 27–31). Paul is here listing certain gifts of ministry which are found in Ephesians 4 as well. He is also adding several other ministry capacities such as the gift of helps and the gift of administration. He clearly teaches that not every ministry gift is for all Christians. Not everyone is a teacher, not everyone is a prophet, etc. But again, Paul strongly indicates that the gifts of ministry are distributed in various ways among all believers. He addresses the Christians of Corinth, not just their main leaders or a certain select group, admonishing them to "*eagerly desire the greater gifts.*"

However, realizing the risk of confusion when a large number of people participate in ministry capacities which give direction and leadership to the Church, Paul also brings strong teaching regarding the need for control and order in the ministry. The risk of disorder was particularly great among the Corinthians who had already shown such tendencies to spiritual immaturity and division. "*What then shall we say, brothers? When you come together, everyone has a hymn, or a word of instruction, a revelation, a tongue, or an interpretation. All of these must be done for the strengthening of the Church . . . But everything should be done in a fitting and orderly way"* (1 Cor. 14:26, 40). The work of the Church should always reflect a variety of ministry as described here by Paul when he instructs the Corinthians regarding their gatherings. And this variety is essential for the building up of the Church. *"All of these must be done for the strengthening of the Church."* It should be strongly emphasized however, that diverse leadership through gifts of ministry distributed among all Christians, should not be taken as a license to allow confusion where everyone goes off and does his own thing. The full width of Jesus' ministry delegated among all believers, can only be realized when everyone submits to Christ's power and authority in His Body with minimal regard to the position of man in this work. Whether one's own or someone else's. There can be no room for the attention-on-man syndrome in the true ministry of the Church.

This broad view of leadership among God's people would release all of us to be part of the ministry of the Church in a new way. This is expressed in Matthew 28 where we are called to participate in the Great Commission. Not just some, while the others give them money to do the job and get reports in monthly newsletters or watch the results on Sunday morning ministry television. Please, don't misunderstand. These works are indeed beneficial to the Church when done in honesty and faithfulness. They should certainly be supported. But the Church must also move in a much broader way—where each member actively participates in the building up of the Body. In fact, we are all through the Great Commission told to teach others in what could be seen as a leadership role. This means of course that we would all be accountable as leaders and must be prepared to share such responsibility as well.

If this in fact is the case, that all Christians walking with the Lord are involved in the ministry offices/gifts, it could change our view of leadership quite a bit. Then your fellow worker at the factory could be a teacher according to Ephesians 4, who might instruct you in the Word of God on Monday afternoon the same way that the pastor would on Sunday morning. And the housewife down the street might speak prophetically to you according to Ephesians 4, just as the well-known prophecy teacher in the widely advertised seminar. This would in no way diminish the work of those whom God has given a highly visible platform to instruct the crowds. But it would broaden the work of the Church when we see that spiritual leadership is a more diverse process where every Christian is involved in one way or the other. Is it possible, by restricting God to the fact that *some* means only a few special ones who carry out spiritual leadership, that we have severely limited His opportunity to build up the Body?

In any event—whether we believe that spiritual leadership is provided on a very broad basis as discussed here, or hold to the more traditional view of a limited number in leadership—it could probably be safely said that spiritual leadership is established on a wider scale than what our current system tends to indicate. This understanding would also counteract the attention-on-man syndrome. We would be less likely to focus on certain people if we understood that leadership is carried out on a much broader basis within the Church.

Submission

This would also have an impact on the area of submission among Christians. The act of submission in its traditional sense, (to yield to the action, control, power of another), is highlighted in Scripture in three particular areas. First, to submit to God. *"Submit yourselves, then, to God. Resist the devil, and he will flee from you. Come near to God, and He will come near to you"* (Jas. 4:7–8). Secondly, submission in marriage. *"Wives, submit to your husbands as to the Lord. For the husband is the head of the wife as Christ is* the Head of the Church . . . Husbands, love your wives, just as Christ loved the Church and gave Himself up for her" (Eph. 5:22–25). Thirdly, submission to government authority. *"Submit your-self for the Lord's sake to every authority instituted among men: whether to the king, as the supreme authority, or to governors, who are sent by him to punish those who do wrong and to commend those who do right"* (1 Pet. 2:13–14).

Submission among the members of the Body of Christ, how-ever, is a somewhat different story. Submission in the Church has a deeper goal and uses a different vehicle than any other of the areas of submission, even that of submission within the marriage. While it's true that the family is an entity built on love and inner strength, it is also a social institution with practical implications for society. That's why we have what we call Christian as well as non-Christian families in the world today. Not so with the Church though. The Church is not a social institution and there really are no churches in the eyes of God other than the true Body of Christ, although some people would like to think so. The Church is an entirely spiritual entity and submission within the Church, while channelled through the members of the Body, should be aimed in one direction only: to the Head, Jesus Christ. *"Submit to one another out of reverence for Christ"* (Eph. 5:21). Not out of rever-ence for other people, leaders, VIPs and celebrities, or organiza-tions and systems. Christ must be the complete center of attention. And the vehicle for this submission is specific and simple: Love. *"A new command I give you: love one another. As I have loved you, so you must love one another. All men will know that you are My disciples if you love one another"* (John 13:34–35). We repeat again, submission within the Church has one goal only—to point to the power and authority of Christ—never to the Church itself or to its leadership. This is where we sometimes go wrong. We think that spiritual submission is displayed well by the power and rulership of God's servants. We rule and are being ruled over by each other instead of submitting in love, which would highlight Christ's work and authority in such a way that the submission part becomes transparent. We also find ourselves right in the middle of the attention-on-man syndrome again.

Since the vehicle for submission in the Church is love, it works differently from other areas of submission required by Scripture. Submission because of love is an entirely different story than submission based on legal requirement. For example, if it says, "No Parking" on the side of the street, you do not necessarily obey the sign because of love for the policeman standing on the street corner looking for someone to catch. Likely, it is quite a selfish motive to avoid a ticket and save money. Many of us Christians would grab a "No Parking" spot in a second if we knew that we wouldn't get caught! Especially if we are late for church service! Our submission to the parking rules is based on the sheer realization that government can come back and punish us if we disobey these rules. There is no motivating love there.

There is some of that involved in our relationship with God as well. We submit to God because He loves us and we love Him. But there is also the addition of reverential fear. We know that He is the ultimate source of love, shown in the sacrifice of Christ. But He is also the ultimate punisher of sin. This gives quite a healthy dose of reverence in our submission to God. Indeed, Scripture specifically instructs us to fear God, which is a good thing. To fear God is not to be afraid of Him but rather to fear doing that which does not please Him. This is why the ultimate act of fearing God is *"to believe in the One He has sent"* (John 6:29), since this is the only way that we can be pleasing in God's sight.

Submission to one another within the Church, however, should be nothing but deep love for everyone who has been placed in the Body of Christ through the new birth in Jesus. Because of this driving force of love, we are willing to receive instruction, discipline, and encouragement from anyone the Lord may choose to use in our lives. It is not threatening since it is carried by love. It will not even be perceived as submission with harsh demands of obedience but rather as a privilege to walk closely with the Lord.

Submission on any other basis will not work. If we decide to submit to certain leadership because of some power and authority in itself, we will be disappointed. Submission by love via the members of the Body should always be seen as submission to Christ's authority. Unfortunately, instead we sometimes have Christians submitting to other Christians, submitting to leaders, submitting to doctrines, submitting to local fellowships, submitting to denominational structures, submitting to great works of God, etc., more than to Christ, the Head.

We repeat, the Lord uses the members of the Body to facilitate correct submission. *"Obey your leaders and submit to their authority. They keep watch over you as men who must give an account"* (Heb. 13:17). But note carefully that we are not to submit to the leaders themselves, but to their authority, which is the property of Christ. When spiritual leadership functions, we obey and submit because these are people who must give an account to Christ. In other words, we are not—and should never be—subject to any man's own power and authority. Only that of Christ. It is possible to receive someone's message and acknowledge that person's part of Jesus' ministry without teaming up with such a person.

Many times we wrongfully feel compelled to recognize and elevate a person simply because God used him for special service. This is not needed, only that we recognize and elevate Christ in the situation. Christ is the leadership, He is the authority, He is the Shepherd of His flock. So, in order for the Body to do its work, there must be great submission to one another *through love.* Then we are truly submitted to Christ and He is free to accomplish His work. The areas of submission are well summarized by the Apostle Peter: *"Show proper respect to everyone: Love the brotherhood of believers, fear God, honor the king"* (1 Pet. 2:17).

Leaders in the New Testament Church are always servants, never kings or rulers. Jesus establishes this in a most wonderful way when He washes His disciples' feet. *"Jesus knew that the Father had put all things under His power, and that He had come from God and was returning to God; so He got up from the meal, took off His outer clothing, and wrapped a towel around His waist. After that, He poured water into a basin and began to wash His disciples feet, drying them with the towel that was wrapped around Him"* (John 13:3–5). Nobody could have argued if Scripture had instead said, *". . . the Father had put all things under His power"* — "so Jesus got up, ordered full attention, demanded special privileges, and made sure that the disciples really knew who was in charge!" Jesus, with His stature and background, certainly could have done this. But He did not. He bowed Himself down in a position of a servant and gave us literally a hands-on lesson regarding leadership and submission in the Church. *"'Do you understand what I have done for you?' He asked them. 'You call Me "Teacher" and "Lord" and rightly so, for that is what I am. Now that I, your Lord and Teacher, have washed your feet, you also should wash one another's feet. I have set you an example that you should do as I have done for you. I tell you the truth, no servant is greater than his master, nor is a messenger greater than the one who sent him. Now that you know these things, you will be blessed if you do them'"* (John 13:12–17).

Do we understand what Jesus did here? He took the attention off His own position by focusing on a great act of servanthood rather than a great act of authority. Yes, He certainly had great authority, but didn't find it necessary to focus on this. And as He said, since we are not greater than He, why should we do anything else? What a blessing for the Church if we can focus on serving one another as He served us instead of focusing on who has power, authority, position, and VIP/ celebrity status.

Man has always had a tendency to be caught up with such things. Either his own power and authority or someone else's. We have already touched on the situation when Jesus told His disciples how He saw Satan fall from heaven like lightning. He said this when the seventy-two disciples returned and expressed their joy that the demons submitted to them in His name. Jesus then further assured them of the authority over the enemy. But He also immediately makes a very important statement. *"However, do not rejoice that the spirits submit to you, but rejoice that your names are written in heaven'"* (Luke 10:20). The disciples returned, focused on the power and authority that they now had in Jesus name. This is so typical. We tend to always become occupied with power, authority, fame, money, or anything else that makes us feel that we are in some sort of control. But Jesus immediately wanted them to re-focus from the area of great power and authority to the fact that they were the object of His great mercy, assuring them of citizenship in the heavenly Kingdom. It is as if Jesus was saying: Watch out! This is the very attitude which got Satan kicked out of heaven.

This is an important lesson for the Church in every generation. Let's not focus on power, authority and position which we ourselves or anyone else might have. Let's be occupied with the great mercy of the Lord without which we would all be lost. Let's focus on His power, His position, His authority, and the fact that we are involved in the work of the Lord by His grace and mercy alone. The Church can never be built up by any other means. We can create impressive human structures by building around the attention on man and his position. We might be able to create financial and statistical success. But we can never build a spiritual house that way. Only if there is a correct view of spiritual leadership, i.e., servanthood and submission to Christ the Head, will the Church be able to *"build itself up in love."*

Whose Ministry, Anyway?

Our view of spiritual leadership is greatly impacted by the way we understand the term "ministry." We often hear phrases like: "So and So's ministry," "my ministry," "her ministry," etc. These types of statements are used today to identify certain things such as a person's calling and specific work, a geographical location of a work, a local church, a non-profit corporation organized according to federal and state laws, etc. However, by identifying a certain work by a person's or organization's name — be it ourselves or others — we many times establish position, power, control, glory, and attention where it does not belong.

Let's look at ministry in the New Testament. *"The point of what we are saying is this: We do have such a high priest, who sat down at the right hand of the throne of the Majesty in heaven, and who serves in the sanctuary, the true tabernacle set up by the Lord, not by man. Every high priest is appointed to offer both gifts and sacrifices, and so it was necessary for this One also to have something to offer . . . But the ministry Jesus has received is as superior to theirs (the high priests of the Old Covenant) as the covenant of which He is mediator is superior to the old one, and is founded on better promises"* (Heb. 8:1–3, 6).

In order to avoid the attention-on-man syndrome in spiritual leadership, it is important that we understand the difference of ministry in the Old and New Covenant. In the Old Covenant, God appointed priests to offer the sacrifices and be the mediators between Him and the people. In the New Covenant, Jesus offered the ultimate sacrifice and became the one and only mediator between God and man. Thus, there is only one ministry in the New Testament Church: Jesus' ministry. Anyone who desires to minister in the New Covenant can do it in one way only: To participate in Jesus' ministry. In the same way that Jesus was on earth a channel for the work of the Father — not His own, so we are today channels for the work of Jesus — not our own. *"The words I say to you are not just My own. Rather, it is the Father, living in Me, who is doing His work"* (John 14:10). It is the Lord living in us doing His work, just like the situation with Jesus and the Father during His time on earth. Not we humans using Him as a booster for our work. Only one can truly say, "My" ministry: Jesus.

Sometimes we act as if God has hired a number of managers to run different departments of His work and has given them almost unlimited authority to act as they see fit. This is not a correct view. All authority in heaven and on earth has been given to Jesus—so it's already gone. There is really no authority left for us. We can only exercise authority when we participate in His authority. We can only minister when we participate in His ministry. Not even our day to day work is our own doing. *"For we are God's workmanship, created in Christ Jesus to do good works, which God prepared in advance for us to do"* (Eph. 2:10). This well-known scripture does not say that God created us so that we could do a good work for Him through our ministry. It means that God has already created good works and we can participate in them if we yield to the ministry of Jesus. Even if we are to be the head of the world's largest "ministry" organization, we still must have the view that we are nothing, have nothing, and control nothing. We are only participating in the ministry of Jesus Christ.

When we understand this very important feature of the New Covenant, we will be able to turn our attention from man to where it should be—on the Minister Himself. Then the fact that the Lord chooses to use people in different ways and on different levels becomes much less of an issue. We will instead focus on His ministry—not man's particular part of it. We will also be open to and happy about the fact that God at any time may do something "greater" through someone else other than our work, our group, or our church. We must not be jealous or competitive in such a situation but rather thank God for this work and bless it in His name. Anyone who is not proceeding with such an attitude cannot be a true leader in the Church. And Christians who are so fixated with certain leaders that they cannot truly rejoice over God's work through others since "their man" was not in the center, will miss much of God's plan for His Church.

Granted, from time to time expressions like "my ministry" are used by God's servants even in scripture. One such example is found in Romans. "*I am talking to you Gentiles. Inasmuch as I am the apostle to the Gentiles, I make much of my ministry in the hope that I may somehow arouse my own people to envy and save some of them*" (Rom. 11:13–14). Paul, known to use many different methods of evangelization, is in this situation highlighting "his" ministry for one reason only: To try to provoke envy among the Jews so that they may seek what has now been offered to the Gentiles. He "proudly" points to himself as having a significant part in proclaiming salvation to the Gentiles, hoping that his fellow Jews would become envious of the Gentiles and seek the gift of salvation through Christ for themselves. In no way is he trying to establish "his" ministry, meaning special authority and position for himself, but rather "making much" of his part of the ministry of Jesus.

Note also that this is done in connection with non-believing Jews, who wouldn't understand the specifics of Jesus' ministry anyway. Non-believers often think that God's servants have some kind of power and control in themselves, since they don't understand Christ's role behind all such work. It would be difficult for them to grasp the correct relationship between Christ and His servants when there is no basis for spiritual discernment and wisdom in their lives. It would be like trying to explain mortgage payments, bank liens, and foreclosure clauses to small children in order to make them understand that your home really belongs to the bank even though you occupy it every day. You might as well call it "my house" since they wouldn't understand much else. However, when addressing believers regarding the spiritual realm, Paul always indicates that by grace alone is he part of the ministry of Christ, who has made the full payment and owns all the property involved. "*Not that we are competent in ourselves to claim anything for ourselves, but our competence comes from God. He has made us competent as ministers of a new covenant—not of the letter but of the Spirit*" (2 Cor. 3:5–6).

The ministry for all believers in the New Covenant is to serve in the ministry of Jesus. We cannot have a "ministry" of our own but we can serve as ministers in His ministry. We can participate in His power and authority but never claim it or use it as our own property. Although expressions like "my ministry" are sometimes used in the New Testament to identify a person's specific work, the Apostle Paul and others were fully aware that they were part of Jesus' ministry only. Not established in some position of authority in themselves. Paul strongly indicates the foolishness of lifting up one's own attributes in this respect, even though he himself does this occasionally. *"Since many are boasting in the way the world does, I too will boast . . . What anyone else dares to boast about—I'm speaking as a fool—I also dare to boast about. Are they Hebrews? So am I. Are they Israelites? So am I. Are they Abraham's descendants? So am I. Are they servants of Christ? (I am out of my mind talking like this.) I am more . . ."* (2 Cor. 11:18, 21–23). Paul indicates very clearly that it is worldly and foolish to try to establish ministry rank and position among men in the work of Jesus. We are all participants in His ministry by His grace. Not by merit or by having earned certain authority for ourselves.

The correct perception of Christians as ministers is outlined well in 2 Corinthians. *"All this is from God, who reconciled us to Himself through Christ and gave us the ministry of reconciliation: that God was reconciling the world to Himself in Christ, not counting men's sin against them. And He has committed to us the message of reconciliation. We are therefore Christ's ambassadors, as though God was making His appeal through us. We implore you on Christ's behalf: be reconciled to God"* (2 Cor. 5:18). We are all ambassadors of Christ, representatives of His ministry, and He speaks through us. We minister on Christ's behalf, not on the basis of our own power, position, or control. This is precisely the ministry of the New Covenant, involving all followers of Christ as servants and ministers in Him.

We want to emphasize again that only Jesus can truly say "My" ministry. And He invites the whole Body of Christ to participate in this ministry. Contrary to the common view that those currently called evangelists, pastors, teachers, etc., are the ones doing the spiritual work while the rest of the Church basically supports them in "their" ministry, these are mainly instructors to engage and prepare all God's people to do the ministry work. "*. . . and some to be pastors and teachers, to prepare God's people for works of service . . .*" Again, the ministry belongs to Jesus, and the work of the ministry is done by the whole Church. Not just a few "special" men and women. We must understand this clearly in order to re-focus from man and put the attention on the Head where it belongs. On this basis, Christ elects to use Christians as He sees fit in His ministry. "*Does not the potter have the right to make out of the same lump of clay some pottery for noble purposes and some for common use?*" (Rom. 9:21). We are of the "same clay," although the Potter elects to form us differently for different uses.

This leads us to another important understanding. In the Old Covenant when Moses had explained the law to the people and the importance of the blood covenant, it says: "*Moreover he sprinkled with blood both the tabernacle, and all the vessels of the ministry*" (Heb. 9:21 KJV). Blood was used to ratify the Old Covenant, sprinkled on the people, the tabernacle, the vessels of ministry, etc. However, when the high priest once a year entered the Holy of Holies on the Day of Atonement to offer the blood of the sacrifice and burn incense, the people had to remain in the outer court. Only vessels needed to perform these duties could be with the high priest inside the veil.

It is different under the New Covenant. "*Therefore, brothers, since we have confidence to enter the Most Holy Place by the blood of Jesus, by a new and living way opened for us through the curtain, that is, His body, and since we have a great Priest over the house of God, let us draw near to God with a sincere heart in full assurance of faith, having our hearts sprinkled to cleanse us from*

a guilty conscience and having our bodies washed with pure water"
(Heb. 10:19–22).

We are now the vessels of Jesus' high priestly ministry and
can enter the Holy of Holies, sprinkled with His blood. Such
vessels are essential for His ministry in the New Covenant, just
as the vessels of ministry were needed for the high priest to perform his duties in the Old Covenant. This was revealed to the
Apostle Paul right after his conversion when God instructed
Ananias to bring a message to him. *"But the Lord said unto him;
Go thy way for he (Paul) is a chosen vessel unto Me, to bear My
name before the Gentiles, and kings and the children of Israel"*
(Acts 9:15 KJV).

A vessel is simply a container to hold substance that does not
come from itself. This is a very important understanding as we try
to de-mask the attention-on-man syndrome. The One who fills
and uses the vessel is to be focused on. Not the vessel itself, even if
it has been formed for a more honorable use. By grace, we are the
vessels of Jesus' ministry. Instead of focusing on "our" ministry in
and through Him, we should place great emphasis on His ministry in and through us.

Fellow Elders

Effective leadership is very important for the Church and we
are not trying to suggest anything else. But we emphasize that in
order for spiritual leadership to succeed, it must steer clear of the
attention-on-man syndrome. Otherwise we will only have a divided
Body filled with competition and quest for power, which unfortunately is the case many times. This has a lot to do with how
leadership views itself, as well as how leadership is being viewed
by those being led. The Apostle Peter addresses other leaders in a
way that could be a model for all spiritual leadership. *"To the
elders among you, I appeal as a fellow elder, a witness of Christ's*

sufferings and one who also will share in the glory to be revealed: Be shepherds of God's flock that is under your care, serving as overseers—not because you must but because you are willing, as God wants you to be; not greedy for money, but eager to serve; not lording it over those entrusted to you, but being examples to the flock. And when the Chief Shepherd appears, you will receive the crown of glory that will never fade away" (1 Pet. 5:1–4).

It should be noted that among the leadership offices in the New Testament Church, that of the elder carries more of an overseeing, or if you will, "ruling" authority. *"Let the elders that rule well be counted worthy of double honor, especially they who labor in the word and doctrine"* (1 Tim. 5:17 KJV). The vehicle God is using to direct the Church from a governing position is the eldership. This is why there are strict qualifications for people in this leadership role. *"An elder must be blameless, the husband of but one wife, a man whose children believe and are not open to the charge of being wild and disobedient. Since an overseer is entrusted with God's work, he must be blameless—not overbearing, not quick-tempered, not given to drunkenness, not violent, not pursuing dishonest gain. Rather he must be hospitable, one who loves what is good, who is self-controlled, upright, holy and disciplined. He must hold firmly to the trustworthy message as it has been taught, so that he can encourage others by sound doctrine and refute those who oppose it"* (Titus 1:6–9). It is also interesting to note that while God appoints leadership in the form of apostles, teachers, prophets, etc., given as gifts to the Church without man's election or approval, man himself is allowed to appoint elders. *"Paul and Barnabas appointed elders for them in each church and, with prayer and fasting, committed them to the Lord in whom they had put their trust"* (Acts 14:23). The Lord knows that His Church will exist in a practical and material world where there is a need for certain visible, authoritative leadership. It appears that He has intended this role for the elders and that we are allowed to appoint these ourselves based on certain common spiritual sense. But the vessels of Christ's ministry, relating mainly to the spiritual building up of the Body of Christ, He appoints, forms, and uses in any way He pleases without prior approval of man. Granted, of course, the elders would also be involved in the ministry offices of evangelists, pastors, teachers, etc., and vice versa.

Peter presents himself as a "fellow elder" to the Christians of Asia Minor. This could be used as an appropriate label for all authoritative leadership among Christians. If any person within the Church should ever look at himself or herself as having any kind of "ruling" power, it should be as a "fellow elder," meaning one among many elders. And the collective leadership of the Church should in this respect look upon itself as "fellow elders," which the Apostle Peter so wisely used in his letter. This is also the way authoritative leadership should be viewed by all Christians: as "fellow elders," whether on a local, national or international level. This will effectively counteract the attention-on-man syndrome, since leadership through "fellow elders" is spread out on a broad enough basis to take focus off any one particular person and prevent kingdom building around "special" human beings. This expression implies leadership by many, which is exactly what God wants. It would also easily take care of those who have started Christian works simply because they would want to see themselves as a great leader with a big platform. They would soon get tired and dry up when treated as just one among all other "fellow elders" of the Church.

There is another interesting and somewhat sensitive question involved here. Should the "fellow elder" perception apply practically to the local church as well in a greater way than what currently is the case? Are we in fact even contributing to the attention-on-man syndrome by putting so much emphasis on the head pastor/elder of a local church and his role in Jesus' ministry? Remember, it isn't his ministry—it's Jesus'. Are we possibly hindering the fullness of the Lord's ministry by excessive focus on a favorite vessel in local churches?

Let's face it, many Christians attend a certain church because they like the pastor. This does not mean that the pastor shouldn't be appreciated and that his role isn't important. It certainly is. But if he becomes the focal point of the church, we again slip back into the attention-on-man syndrome. The different offices of Jesus' ministry; apostles, teachers, prophets, etc., have been given to bring balance to the Church. Over-emphasis on any one particular of the leadership offices will throw the Church off balance. This would also apply very much to the office of the pastor.

One way to prevent this is to look at local spiritual leadership in the broader, "fellow elder" sense, where many have the same role and authority so that no one in particular will be elevated and given undue attention. When we understand that Christ has delegated His authority to many—even in the local church—who would equally share a main leadership role and responsibility, it helps to prevent personality attachment which can create wrongful focus on man. The Church would also avoid many problems which happen if the one "main" leader falls or is unable to lead for some other reason. Since everything was built up around him, everything will also come crashing down around him. This can largely be avoided by applying the "fellow elder" concept to any type of Christian work so that there are others to keep the work going with minor interruptions in case of such problems.

There are many more pastors than just those who occupy church pulpits on Sunday morning and sign checks for non-profit corporations. For example, every Christian husband should see himself as the pastor of his household. There are also many more teachers, etc., than just those who labor fulltime in Christian work. This is an important understanding which determines the maturity of the Body of Christ in the world today. We need to avoid undue attachment to certain messengers, their names, preaching style, organizations, etc., so that the ministry of Christ may flow freely through His Body.

It is a fact that many Christians identify themselves by whose church they attend, whose doctrine they believe in, the name of a denomination, whose ministry they support, whose preaching style they like, etc., and not simply as followers of Christ. This has created a wrongful focus on the vessels of ministry rather than the Minister Himself who uses the vessels of ministry in His work. Christ is the Head of the Church, the King of the Kingdom, the Minister of the New Covenant and the Shepherd of His flock. By grace, He uses vessels like you and me for the purposes of His ministry. But these vessels are not to be given undue attention—no matter who they are!

With this view in mind (and spirit!), we can take the attention off individual leaders and turn it on to Christ where it belongs. Leadership in the Church is completely top-centered, directed exclusively from the Head. And the Lord delegates His leadership authority in such a broad way that it is inappropriate to focus on specific individuals or favorite "vessels" within Church leadership. If we do so, we are violating the very principles of the Body as they are implemented by Christ.

Spiritual Authority

The area of spiritual authority is widely discussed as it pertains to spiritual leadership. We should repeat what we stated earlier, that man can really have no authority in himself, only participate in Christ's authority. Jesus said: *"All authority in heaven and on earth has been given to Me."* So all of it is gone. There is nothing left for man to take other than to participate in Christ's complete authority. This is a very important understanding for the Church and will do away with the false impression that authority, delegated by Christ to man, somehow becomes our property to use in our own discretion. Remember, we participate in the work of the Lord as vessels in His ministry, not as managers or controllers of some of His departments. Not as kings, rulers, or any other title that might imply authority on earth.

Let's look at some areas which wrongfully have become measuring sticks of spiritual authority. The most obvious is the area of numbers and statistics. The Church has, to a great extent, adopted an incorrect view that growing numbers and statistics are true evidence of God's blessing and genuine, spiritual authority at work. The size of churches and ministries, growth of denominations, attendance records, how much money raised, number of books sold, number of conversions, etc., seem to play an overwhelming role in our perceived understanding of what God is or isn't doing. For example, when we look for spiritual authority among the leadership, we often determine that the pastor with the biggest church, the teacher pulling the largest crowds, etc., has the highest authority. That's just about a given today. If someone has a "successful ministry" numbers-wise, we often conclude that he has the authority of the Lord. And the larger the "ministry" the greater the authority!

This is an incorrect view. Authority does not come from good statistics or numbers. Nor are these necessarily a reflection of spiritual authority. Authority comes from Christ whose definition of success and effectiveness is entirely different from the world's point of view. It is often quite unclear which definition we are applying in the Church — Christ's or the world's? It seems that our most important column on the scale of success is called *quantity*. God's most important column is called *quality*. And in our eagerness to reach high on the scale of quantity, we often do damage to the measurement of quality. By working hard to produce quantity, God's Kingdom seemingly moves forward strongly. However, this may not at all be the case measured from the point of spiritual quality. We might even be backtracking right in the middle of our glorious statistics. This does not mean that smaller numbers are more spiritual. God desires to expand His Church to include everyone, producing numbers and statistics bigger than we can imagine. However, the kind of measurements we use to evaluate and receive authority will determine whether or not such expansion can take place. If we are blinded and unable to receive true spiritual authority where the Lord has placed it—because we constantly look for worldly attributes such as numbers, statistics, and VIP status—we will not understand His ways and will miss His perfect plan. The Lord will then have to keep working with what could be called His Plan B, a modified version of His perfect plan. Thank God that He does! But this is not what He truly prefers.

One thing should be clearly understood regarding the numbers and statistics we keep. They are all basically incorrect! Only God knows the number of Christians in the world. Only God knows how many are truly born again in a local church. Only God knows how many really gave their hearts to Christ in a revival meeting. Only God knows how many names are written in the Lamb's Book of Life. Our numbers are nothing but wild and sometimes worldly guesses. (To enhance our reputation in front of each other!) We are in danger of presenting lies and falsehoods every time we quote numbers and statistics based on our view and understanding. God evaluates things from a clear, spiritual perspective and only He can determine the real facts. Sometimes we use expressions like: "Heaven will show the true result." Yes, that is absolutely right. The only problem is that we mainly use such statements when our numbers are low and unattractive. If we think we have some magnificent statistics to present, we certainly don't wait until we get to heaven! We immediately proclaim them in bold headlines everywhere. However, we must learn to hand over the analysis of all this to the Lord since our numbers are incorrect anyway. They should not be used as a measuring stick of spiritual authority.

Another area of questionable measurement of spiritual authority is found in the amount and intensity of words and messages being communicated through the Church. With the help of modern communications, countless messages from the Church can now reach farther through radio, television, books, magazines, cassettes, music, church services, seminars, concerts, conferences, etc., than in any other time of history. In fact, one preacher alone can today reach more people by radio or television in a half-hour than all of Jesus' twelve disciples combined during their entire lifetime. By all rights, the world should have been completely saved and restored several times over by now! This extensive and powerful communications ability often leads us to believe that there must be spiritual authority involved. Just like the saying: "If it's printed in the paper, it must be true!" Not necessarily so. The ability to proclaim words and messages does not automatically ensure spiritual authority. And all these messages are sometimes so contradictory that God would appear to be an old, senile man on His golden rocking chair in heaven, who forgets from one hour to the next what He has said before! If everything labeled a word from God actually was a word from Him, we would have to conclude that our God is quite confused. Not so, of course. The problem lies on our side, where we often are so busy keeping this vast communications machinery going that we do not take the time to understand the origin, importance, and application of true spiritual authority.

It is quite interesting what was said about Jesus: "*. . . the crowds were amazed at His teaching, because He taught as one who had authority, and not as their teachers of the law*" (Matt. 7:28–29). Jesus probably looked like any other teacher of His day, spoke many of the same words and quoted the same Old Testament scriptures. But something was different and went right to the heart of the listeners. He had spiritual authority, unlike the others. Unless the Church communicates in the power of that same authority from Him, it will be nothing but a gigantic, man-made word processor. Then speaking ability, musical talent, theological education, charm and wit, stage presence, and other human attributes become substitutes for spiritual authority. Again, we are not saying that God cannot use such gifts. But it must be clearly understood that these things in themselves have nothing to do with spiritual authority. Spiritual authority comes about when Christ in His eternal plan uses man to reach out with His ministry. He might very well use persons with great gifts and talents. He might just as well use those with none of the above. Spiritual authority is only in effect when He does His work—not when we do ours. Only when Christ speaks His word—not when we speak ours, even though our words might be filled with "spiritual" facts and religious theories. It should be clearly understood that the ability to produce words, which the Church is doing in such abundance today, does not necessarily stand for spiritual authority.

We must be aware of how dangerous the attention-on-man syndrome is in the area of spiritual leadership. In its full-grown form, it will make us completely misjudge spiritual authority. Our inner sight cannot stay clear if it is clouded by focus on the success, impressive statistics, special abilities, emotional expressions, convincing words, or VIP status of certain men and women. Leaders in the Church must not be evaluated in the same way as leaders in the world. Spiritual authority begins and ends with Christ. Human beings are only channels to facilitate His authority. Undue focus on man damages this authority. Such damage must be prevented by the understanding and turning away from the attention-on-man syndrome.

Gifts and Talents

In order to better understand spiritual authority and leadership, we need to also fine-tune our understanding regarding natural gifts and talents versus spiritual gifts. There is often great confusion in this area. Just about every person has a natural talent for something. Some have talents that shine greatly above everyone else, particularly in areas such as drama, music, arts, etc. This has really nothing to do with God in their lives other than the fact that every human is a result of His creation, and the makeup of everyone's being in essence comes from Him. Many of the most talented people throughout history have been non-Christians and the fact that they did not surrender to the Lord did not revoke their natural gifts and talents. There is nothing wrong with these natural gifts. God wants us to enjoy the fruit of the natural talents. However, there is sometimes great confusion in the Church regarding the priority order and usage of such talents. Remember that the main mission of the Church is to convey realities in the spiritual realm, not the natural. *"His intent was that now, through the Church, the manifold wisdom of God should be made known to the rulers and authorities in the Heavenly realms, according to His eternal purpose which He accomplished in Christ Jesus our Lord "* (Eph. 3:10–11). The work which is to be done in the spiritual realm has to be accomplished through spiritual understanding, spiritual weapons, and spiritual offices/ gifts. Natural talents are of no value to God unless they simply become a vehicle for true spiritual gifts and are placed in their correct priority order. This is where the Church is often confused, putting such emphasis on the natural talents that there sometimes is hardly even a search for spiritual gifts and the ministry of Christ.

Spiritual gifts are diverse and given to each member of the Body of Christ. *"There are different kinds of gifts, but the same Spirit. There are different kinds of service, but the same Lord. There are different kinds of working, but the same God works all of them in all men"* (1 Cor. 12:4–6). Spiritual gifts function in a different realm and in a different way than natural talents. The Apostle Paul brings an interesting analysis earlier in the same chapter. *"Now about spiritual gifts, brothers, I do not want you to be ignorant. You know that when you were pagans, somehow or other you were influenced and led astray to dumb idols. Therefore I tell you that no one who is speaking by the Spirit of God says, 'Jesus be cursed,' and no one can say, 'Jesus is Lord,' except by the Holy Spirit"* (1 Cor. 12:1–3). It is not the words or expressions but the reality behind them which is important. Anyone can say "Jesus is Lord." It is just three words and anyone with the gift of speaking can say it. But no one can say "Jesus is Lord" and *express the reality of it* without God's Spirit and His gifts. There is no magic power in the words themselves. If so, Paul would be in great trouble here since he just said "Jesus be cursed." The spiritual reality behind words and deeds is what counts. It is extremely important to understand that spiritual reality can only be expressed through spiritual gifts—not mere natural talents. These are the gifts and workings which are to be prioritized in the Church. Not the natural talents, although these many times serve as channels to express true spiritual gifts.

Focus on natural talents leads to focus on man and we step right in to the attention-on-man syndrome. Focus on spiritual gifts leads us to God and we effectively avoid this syndrome. However, even though we might understand the priority of spiritual gifts, Let's not fall into the trap of thinking that God is dependent on the natural talents in order for the spiritual gifts to be displayed correctly. God can work perfectly through someone with no talents. In fact, sometimes He even arranges to put aside the natural talent so that what is done by the Spirit will not be tainted by the flesh. Remember Moses as a prince in Egypt. *"Moses was educated in all the wisdom of the Egyptians and was powerful in speech and action"* (Acts 7:22). Here we see great natural talent and ability at play. But listen to what happened when God had trained him as a shepherd in the desert for several years and came back at the burning bush to call him as the deliverer of the Israelites. *"O Lord, I have never been eloquent, neither in the past nor since You have spoken to Your servant. I am slow in speech and tongue"* (Exod. 4:10). And so deep was his lack of trust now in his own ability that God had to give him Aaron as a spokesman. The emphasis on natural ability was gone, and now God could really use him. It is interesting to note—especially today when we're always looking for a good speaker— that Moses at first was a good speaker but had to become a less good one in order for God to use him. Is it possible that the speaking ability of men and women sometimes even hinders God's work? Simply because we have a tendency to focus on that very ability instead of the message, even though the message might be a true word from God. We walk away thinking about what a great speaker we have heard, instead of thinking about a great word from a great God, with no special regard to the channel He spoke through.

The platform messengers must be especially alert in this area. Anything done in the name of the Lord with the intent to display one's natural talent and impress the listeners on that level, is not pleasing to Him. Jesus spoke very strong words regarding those who want to show off. *"While all the people were listening, Jesus said to His disciples, 'Beware of the teachers of the law. They like to walk around in flowing robes and love to be greeted in the market places and have the most important seats in the synagogues and the places of honor at banquets. They devour widows' houses and for a show make lengthy prayers. Such men will be punished most severely'"* (Luke 20:45–47). The Lord is greatly bothered by anything done in His name *"for a show."* And the Church continues to fall into this trap. Sometimes, stunning sermons have been preached—for a show. Standing-ovation-type songs have been sung—for a show. Remarkable testimonies of miracles and signs have been presented—for a show. Spectacular meetings and magnificent programs have been put together—for a show. We can only comment with Jesus' own words. We will be *"punished most severely"* if this is our behavior. The show mentality in the Church is in direct league with the flesh, assisted by the attention-on-man syndrome. And the flesh thrives on natural talents and abilities.

Yes, this is an area where the platform messengers need to be very careful. But so must the audience as well. As stated above, God is not pleased with a show-off mentality among leadership in the Church. Neither is He pleased with cravings for spectacular natural talent and sensational show-offs that sometimes exist among the flock. Maybe even to the point of full-fledged idolatry if we worship the natural talents of His messengers. This is an abomination in His sight. Whatever happened to good, old Christianity and the simple message of the crucified and resurrected Savior with no influence from Hollywood, Madison Avenue, or 666 Flashy Street right around the corner from 1 Fleshy Place!? That's where we will end up unless we turn our focus totally on Christ and renounce the world's attitude in this respect.

Another important point should be clearly understood. When evaluating God's servants in terms of quality of service, etc., this should certainly not be done from the perspective of natural talent—nor just spiritual gifts alone—but rather from the perspective of spiritual fruit. Jesus makes the following statement when He warns about false prophets. *"By their fruit you will recognize them"* (*"know them,"* KJV) (Matt. 7:16). Sometimes we are also confused regarding spiritual fruit versus spiritual gifts. It is a common misunderstanding to think that fruit is defined by one's hard labor, ability to produce tangible results, number of souls won, etc. Not so. Instead, spiritual fruit is basically the fruit of the Spirit in our inner being. It is the attitude and mind of Christ, more and more taking over our carnal self. It is love, meekness, patience, humility, and the like growing within. This is what is to be analyzed when we look at the quality of any servant. Not his ability to speak eloquently, produce great outward movement, effectively raise funds, etc. Nor the fact that he might be equipped with great spiritual gifts. Jesus instructed us to evaluate the fruit simply because this is the only way we will have a true measurement. Many false prophets and carnal people have produced great outward results and shown extreme effectiveness in their labor. But only those walking close to the Lord in His truth can produce genuine spiritual fruit in the form of love, peace, patience, self control, etc. This is why it is so important to evaluate any work—not first by visible motion, numbers, statistics and outward effectiveness—but by the inward spiritual fruit of those involved. Even if great spiritual gifts are present, the evaluation of spiritual fruit should still be the measuring stick.

The Church has missed out on God's work many times because of the confusion regarding natural talents versus spiritual gifts. We have also missed God, although we might understand the importance and priority of spiritual gifts, because of the wrongful belief that these gifts are best used with a healthy dose of natural talent. We really like it when God sends someone with great spiritual understanding and gifts together with great natural talents; speaking ability, musical talent, etc. But we are not as interested when He sends someone with spiritual gifts only, and just about no natural talents. That might be harmful to attendance records and the reputation of local churches, conferences and seminars! This has to do with our tendency today in the Church to prioritize so called "Event Christianity," which we will discuss later.

It is so easy to be focused on man's natural abilities and outward appearance. Even some of God's "finest" servants fall into this trap now and then. One such example is the situation when God had rejected King Saul and instructed Samuel to go to Bethlehem to anoint one of Jesse's sons as the new king. *"Then he consecrated Jesse and his sons and invited them to the sacrifice. When they arrived, Samuel saw Eliab and thought, 'Surely the Lord's anointed stands here before the Lord.' But the Lord said to Samuel, 'Do not consider his appearance or his height, for I have rejected him. The Lord does not look at the things man looks at. Man looks at the outward appearance, but the Lord looks at the heart'"* (1 Sam. 16:5–7).

This is a typical situation where God's view and man's view do not correspond. Samuel was obviously quite impressed with the outward stature of Eliab and immediately came to the conclusion that God would use him. But God says specifically to not consider *"appearance"* or *"height."* These are the very things we tend to focus on, whether in the form of physical appearance, natural abilities, VIP status, social prominence, or similar traits. This in-struction would apply even stronger in the New Covenant since God has now revealed the One whose appearance, height, beauty, power, and authority far surpasses anyone or anything else. We must learn to look for His stature and beauty *within the inner man* of other people. Not their outward appearance or natural talents. Only then can we clearly discern whom God has chosen to use in His work.

Confirmation

A key word to a correct view of leadership in the Church is confirmation. In the Old Covenant, there were kings, prophets, etc., who stood between God and the people. They communicated with God and conveyed His will to others. In the New Covenant, every Christian has a direct line to the heart of God through Jesus. There-fore, the role of spiritual leadership in the Church is mainly to confirm what God is already speaking to His people. A true spiri-tual leader will always strike a chord of harmony with those who are set on following Christ. Such a leader's teaching and actions will be confirmed by the Holy Spirit in the hearts of the flock as the leadership and work of Christ. By this confirmation, the Body of Christ will become more mature and be built up in greater unity for service.

On the other hand, some try to exercise leadership in them-selves and attempt to make others follow, maintaining that they have the "authority" without having received true authority from Christ. The teaching from such persons may be powerful in words and theological understanding, stirring up strong emotions among the listeners. But there is no deep spiritual confirmation within the Body. This is a sure sign that this is not spiritual au-thority in action, but some other kind. The Church has ended up in many confusing situations when people feel emotionally compelled to blindly follow these fast-talking leaders with so-called authority. And most of the time there is great emphasis on the leader himself, whereas true spiritual leadership actively tries to stay in the background so that Christ may be clearly seen.

In order to correctly discern spiritual leadership, we must deal with the attention-on-man syndrome. It is very easy to be fooled in the spiritual confirmation process if someone with overwhelming VIP credentials shows up. Let's not mistake spiritual authority instituted by Christ for high visibility, speaking talent, and other things that might attract a crowd. This is not to say that these kinds of gifts and talents cannot be used by the Lord in spiritual leadership. But we must always start to look for spiritual leadership from the other direction—beginning with Christ—not man. This is where the confirmation process in our hearts is so important.

Wrongful focus on man is also evidence of immaturity in the Church. When we are fixated on God's messengers, we still have a need to grow into maturity in Christ. The messengers are so interesting to us simply because we have not fully seen Christ in all His glory. We have not yet moved so close to Him that everyone else fades out of view. Mature Christians have learned to look to Christ first and see God's messengers only as conduits for Christ's word and actions. Such Christians have a very easy time with the confirmation process. This is called spiritual discernment; to be able to analyze and understand what God is or isn't doing. The attention-on-man syndrome severely hinders spiritual discernment and will keep Christians in a state of immaturity, if allowed to prevail.

The confirmation and exercise of authority in the Kingdom of God is done quite differently than in the world. Jesus emphasized a very important point during the Last Supper. *"The kings of the Gentiles lord it over them; and those who exercise authority over them call themselves Benefactors. But you are not to be like that. Instead, the greatest among you should be like the youngest, and the one who rules like the one who serves"* (Luke 22:25–26). The key point here is illustrated by the word "benefactor." A benefactor is one who gives gifts for the benefit of others who then become the beneficiaries. In other words, it is a person doing good towards others. However, he does it out of a position of power and control. He might control money and other assets which he can, in his own discretion, give to others. And Jesus says very clearly: *"But you are not to be like that."* This is the way authority is defined in the world, but it is not the way it is supposed to be done in the Kingdom of God. No man can exercise spiritual authority out of a position of power and control. *"Instead, the greatest among you should be like the youngest, and the one who rules, like the one who serves."* There is only one Benefactor in the Kingdom of God, Jesus Christ. Spiritual authority and spiritual gifts are not really vested in men, only communicated through man by Him. This is an important understanding as we strive to pull away from the attention-on-man syndrome and its negative impact on the Church.

Old Testament Leadership

There is an interesting lesson regarding Old Testament leadership which might explain why we are so bent on focusing on man in the work of God. The elders of Israel came to Samuel one day with the following message: *"'You are old, and your sons do not walk in your ways; now appoint a king to lead us, such as all the other nations have.' But when they said, 'Give us a king to lead us,' this displeased Samuel; so he prayed to the Lord. And the Lord told him: 'Listen to all that the people are saying to you; it is not you they have rejected, but they have rejected Me as their king. As they have done from the day I brought them up out of Egypt until this day, forsaking Me and serving other gods, so they are doing to you. Now listen to them; but warn them solemnly and let them know what the king who will reign over them will do'"* (1 Sam. 8:5–9).

It appears that it really wasn't God's perfect will that Israel should have a king. Even after the appointment of the king, Samuel strongly chastised the people for their request. *"And you will realize what an evil thing you did in the eyes of the Lord when you asked for a king"* (1 Sam. 12:17). God was to be their King and their only Source, which would also further establish that Israel was called by the Almighty and thus different from all other nations. However, the people had a different idea. They wanted to be like the rest of the world with their own king. This is basically what transpires with the temptation to focus on man in the Church. Samuel took this request to the Lord, who made it very clear that this was a flat rejection of Him as their King. Interestingly, God instructed Samuel to still listen to the request but strongly warn the people regarding the consequences. Their sons and their daughters would have to serve the king by working in his stables, in his palace, and in his weapon factories. A king would tax the people in different ways, make some into slaves, and take the best of their cattle. God wanted the people to be fully aware of what they were asking for, knowing that they would be tired of this some day. *"When that day comes, you will cry out for relief from the king you have chosen, and the Lord will not answer you in that day"* (1 Sam. 8:18). Despite the clear understanding that God was not pleased with their request and the stern warning of what would happen, the people still stood firm in their wishes. *"But the people refused to listen to Samuel. 'No!' they said. 'We want a king over us. Then we will be like all the other nations, with a king to lead us and go out before us and fight our battles'"* (1 Sam. 8:19–20).

It seems there were several specific reasons why they absolutely wanted a king. First, so that they could be *"like all the other nations."* One of God's big problems, both in the Old and the New Covenant, has been to keep His people separate and different from the world. God's people have always been tempted to want to be like the world. This is very apparent with regards to the attention-on-man syndrome. We would simply rather take our lead from the secular world; politics, the entertainment industry, etc., and structure ourselves in a similar manner instead of being different and set apart according to God's ways.

God did not abandon the Israelites because of this request. Instead, He even blessed them greatly. And neither is He abandoning the Church because of wrongful focus on man. But it should be clearly understood that this is not His perfect plan. God's blessing is not His stamp of approval on man's ways and attitudes. His blessing is only evidence of His unmerited grace and that He does His work *in spite* of us. Never fall for the heresy that if God is blessing the work through some person or organization, they are more "right" than others, or even "right" at all. The Israelites walked forty years in the desert experiencing daily miracles in the form of manna from heaven, healing from sicknesses, etc., as evidence of God's presence. But, in a sense, they were on the wrong track the whole time! By disbelief, they had neglected to enter the Promised Land according to God's perfect plan. God continued His work with them anyway by His great mercy, even though at one point He came quite close to abandoning the Israelites and Moses had to intercede with God on behalf of the people. The grace of God is displayed in Israel's walk. Not that they earned manna from heaven because of their own works or worthiness. Quite the contrary.

In the same way, when Israel asked for a king, they displayed blatant dissatisfaction with the Lord and a desire to be like the rest of the world. But God still continued to work with them because of His great mercy. When God works, it is always because He has chosen to do so based solely on His will and plan. Never because man has earned a certain status or has become good enough in himself to do "great" things. God always works in spite of us, although it gives Him great joy when He finds someone "after His own heart" who fully agrees with His plan and becomes most useful to God.

The Church is constantly tempted to conform to the world. It is so easy to look for kings *"just like the other nations."* By doing so, we are in danger of having rejected God as our King, just like the Israelites.

Another reason why the Israelites wanted a king is also quite obvious. *". . . a king **to lead us**,"* (KJV: *"to judge us"*) Preceding this request were years of battles with the Philistines who later returned the ark of the Lord, and were finally defeated under the leadership of Samuel. These were years of great travail for the people of Israel. *"It was a long time, twenty years in all, that the ark remained at Kiriath Jearim, and all the people of Israel mourned and sought after the Lord"* (1 Sam. 7:2). It was probably with this in mind, and seeing that Samuel was old and would soon leave them, that they made their request for a king. They were tired of having to travail and seek the Lord for themselves. Let someone else do this for us! This is typical for God's people even today. Let's get a "king" who will do the deep and hard seeking. Then we don't need to take as much responsibility and can always blame the "king" later if things go wrong! This is a dangerous but common attitude. Not only does God want us to steer clear of the attention on man in order to avoid idolatry. He also wants all of His children to seek Him deeply and hear from Him for themselves. God wants each one of the citizens of His Kingdom to take the same responsibility and seek Him for directions.

Israel also asked for a king for the following reason: *". . . to go out before us and **fight our battles**."* They were tired of the responsibility and the fight. They wanted somebody who could plot and scheme for them, handle their battles, and make them a winning people. Does this sound familiar? Let's send our money to So-and-So and let him go out and win the world! Let's have our "kings" fight the battles the Church must face in this world. This is another reason why the attention on man must be put aside. God's army, the Church, has to be engaged fully on every level in order to display Christ's victory. It cannot be done by a few "kings" here and there. Spiritual leadership within the Church is not meant to relieve the rest of the Body from its duty, rather to engage it even more.

There is yet another interesting aspect regarding the kings of the Old Covenant which also has parallels to our time. God made it very clear that if they wanted a king, they would have to accept that he would take the best of their fields and cattle, make their sons and daughters his servants, and in general build wealth and power for himself. These special "perks" go with the territory of a king.

We have a similar situation in the Church today. There are many "kings" who have become used to special perks in the form of fame, influence, control, money, celebrity status, personal recognition, etc., because they have reached a certain VIP level in the Christian community. There are still many thrones to sit on. Not in the form of gold-plated chairs in big palaces. But in the form of church platforms, television visibility, hit songs, best-seller books, awards, and other areas where the attention-on-man syndrome might be in effect. This is not to say that anyone with a big church or other visible position in Christianity views himself as a "king." But the borderline between seeing such a position as an opportunity to serve and glorify the Lord only—as opposed to a throne to reign from—is very fine. Most certainly, anyone with a visible position in the Church will be tempted by Satan to see himself as a king. And it is obvious that we have not always been able to resist that temptation.

It should be clearly understood that the leadership offices in the New Covenant are not to be "enjoyed" for career, popularity, financial gain, or other similar purposes. In fact, anyone serving in these offices will have a life of conflict. Not necessarily in a material sense, but in the sense that he will always battle the enemy. Granted, he will always be victorious in Christ, but not without a fight. Jesus never promised us victory without battles. On the contrary, He assured us that we will have battles and conflicts in this world.

The Apostle Peter is a good example of this. He had failed bitterly. After the resurrection, Jesus reinstates Peter by asking him three times if he loved the Lord. Peter three times had to affirm his love for Jesus, just as he three times had denied Him. Directly thereafter, Jesus gives Peter an outline of his life ahead. "Jesus said, *'Feed My sheep. I tell you the truth, when you were younger you dressed yourself and went where you wanted; but when you are old you will stretch out your hands, and someone else will dress you and lead you where you do not want to go.' Jesus said this to indicate the kind of death by which Peter would glorify God. Then He said to him, 'Follow Me!*(John 21:17–19). Peter had heard the same words, "*Follow Me*" from the same man years earlier when he and his brother Andrew were called by Jesus at the Sea of Galilee. He had been through ups and downs and finds himself called again by the resurrected Jesus. But this time in a much deeper way. Peter was now painfully aware of his own weakness and fully appraised of the cost of following the Lord. Jesus made it clear that he was going to be a martyr. This had a profound effect on his work for the Lord, as he accepted the second call to follow. Peter could not possibly be focused on success, publicity, career, etc. He knew what he had to look forward to. When he preached the powerful sermon on the day of Pentecost—inspiring one of the greatest re-vivals ever—he surely wasn't thinking about how his own name would be displayed in the headlines and his publicity and fame increase as a result of this great success. Instead, he might have suspected that this would be the end, even though Jesus had indi-cated that it would happen in his older days. This kind of bold stand for the Lord could surely trigger the events leading to his martyrdom. He looked over his shoulder, not to see how many news reporters and publicity people were there, but to see where the persecutors were with their chains to bind him and lead him where he didn't want to go. This made Peter a strong and effective servant of God. He worked for the Lord only—not anyone else. Not even his own reputation.

This should always be our attitude whether we have to give our lives in martyrdom or not. We are not placed on earth to make a mark on the history of time, which unfortunately even many Christians spend most of their time trying to do. We are here to make a mark on the history of eternity, which is far different from our history books. And the only way to do this is to closely follow, serve, and glorify the One who Himself is the eternal history.

Back to the Israelites in the Old Covenant. God knew beforehand that once the Israelites would get their kings, they would soon tire of being taxed and ruled by them. There was a very simple solution to this problem—to not have kings at all! The Church needs to heed this warning. Let's turn away from the fractional kingdom building within God's great Kingdom, be it around an individual, a denomination, a particular ministry or whatever. We are one Kingdom with one King, Jesus Christ. Any other view just complicates matters and puts an undue burden on God's people.

A Religious Spirit at Work

There is an additional aspect we must look at with respect to the difference in leadership between the Old and the New Covenant. This particular area can severely hinder the effectiveness of the Church and must be clearly understood. As stated earlier, God used priests, prophets, judges, and kings as middlemen under the Old Covenant. These middlemen received special insight as they heard from God and then in turn communicated God's word to the people. There was no direct line between God and each individual. Communication mainly went through specially appointed people.

In the New Covenant, on the other hand, Christ became the ultimate middleman and opened a new and living way to the heart of God for all who would trust in Him. Each Christian now has a direct connection to God and needs no other mediator. Instead, we are encouraged to put full confidence in Christ's finished work. We refer again to Hebrews 10: *"Therefore, brothers, since we have confidence to enter the Most Holy Place by the blood of Jesus, . . . let us draw near to God with a sincere heart. . . ."* (Heb. 10:19, 22).

It appears, however, that in spite of our faith in Christ's work, we sometimes still try to hold on to the Old Covenant order with regard to leadership. We still look for men and women who seem to be a little closer to God, hear His voice a little clearer, understand His word a little better, and whose prayers seem to reach God a little faster than the rest of us. We often continue to seek priests and prophets according to the old way, not fully understanding that this was done away with in the New Covenant. Though we still have priests and prophets, they now are vessels under Jesus' ministry and not the primary representatives between God and man. And leaders looked upon with Old Testament eyes may not always do everything they can to discourage this either. They might even enjoy the perks of this kind of status. Indeed, there are those who love to be perceived in the same way as the Old Testament prophets. Or it may not be selfish at all. It may simply be a matter of support and survival for a ministry. To be frank, it does wonders for fundraising to have someone at the top who appears to be a little closer to the Lord than anyone else and can supposedly arrange special blessings for the people.

THE FORCE BEHIND ALL THIS IS A RELIGIOUS SPIRIT WHO ATTEMPTS TO BIND THE CHURCH IN THE OLD TESTAMENT BONDAGE OF THE LAW. In fact, this is a very serious situation of major disbelief in the finished work of Christ. We act as if His work was not enough. As if we still need special men and women as additional mediators between God and His Church. If this is our view, we basically disapprove of Jesus' high priestly ministry and fall back into Old Covenant thinking. The Church will then be unable to experience true freedom in Christ. This attitude can be avoided by simply taking a correct view of spiritual leadership in the New Covenant. As stated before, the key word is confirmation. The offices of pastors, teachers, prophets, etc., are instituted to confirm what God is already speaking to each individual who would want to hear from Him. They are not to continue the same role as Old Covenant leadership. Middlemen are no longer needed between God and His people. The offices of leadership in the Church are given to serve and participate in the building up of His Body which receives its instructions and impulses directly from the Head. Any other view will only hinder the growth of the Body and in essence be a disapproval of Jesus' finished work on the cross.

This religious spirit, if allowed to prevail, will also greatly hinder true fellowship in the Body of Christ. If we rally around men and women rather than Christ only, the Holy Spirit will not be able to bring the Church to true oneness. The situation in this respect is also quite different from the Old Covenant. There the people were supposed to rally around leaders to achieve unity. After God reluctantly had given Israel their king, we sometimes find dramatic examples of how such a position was to be the rallying point. This happened once when the Ammonites threatened to bring great disgrace on Israel and word of this came to King Saul. *"When Saul heard their words, the Spirit of God came upon him in power, and he burned with anger. He took a pair of oxen, cut them into pieces, and sent the pieces by messengers throughout Israel, proclaiming, 'This is what will be done to the oxen of anyone who does not follow Saul and Samuel.' Then the terror of the Lord fell on the people, and they turned out as one man"* (1 Sam. 11:6–7).

Talk about an effective strategy for unity! Saul needed the men to meet this threat. And they all turned out as one because the Spirit of the Lord allowed (and inspired!) this kind of action under the Old Covenant. The leaders appointed by God were the rallying points and the mediators between Him and the people. They were sometimes allowed to strongly and dramatically assert themselves, as in this case. They were supposed to be obeyed and focused on. But not so in the New Covenant. Man should never be the rallying point now, whether due to love, threat, guilt, promises of prosperity, or anything else that could round up groups of people. No man is to demand obedience from others in the New Covenant. Christ only can make such demands. He is now the King, the Head, the Centerpoint, and the only One who should say: Follow Me! The "attention on man" attitude in this respect will only allow a religious spirit to interfere with real unity and fellowship in the Body as it is intended by the Lord.

Unity in the Church

There has been endless teaching regarding the need for unity in the Body. Unfortunately though, much of the practical application can be summarized as follows: If everyone lines up behind me, my ministry, my church, my denomination, and my thing— we will all be united! Or the more sophisticated version where a leader sends subtle signals that those who believe in his ministry perhaps shouldn't team up with others as well, but rather pledge ($!!) their loyalty right there with him in order to achieve greater "unity." This is probably the reason why—even after all this talk of unity—the Church is still greatly divided. In spite of all the quotes from John 17, there is still a strong spirit of competition, fueled by many inflated egos among the leadership which lead to strife, in-fighting, and church politics that sometimes are as bad as anything you would see in the world. Many attempt to succeed at the expense of others. All of this is directly related to the attention-on-man syndrome. Leadership is often trying to solidify its position and people are encouraged to "vote" for one or the other. This is just like earthly politics. We do not recognize that there is only one "vote" in the Kingdom—for Christ and no one else. And strangely enough, even the scriptural teaching of unity can be used to secure votes from the people because it sounds like the right thing to say. This is very similar to worldly politics where we are constantly amazed at the difference between the big words and the practical reality behind them.

The Apostle Paul brings powerful teaching to the Corinthians in this respect. He had been informed that there were arguments and divisions among them and they sided with different leaders. *"What I mean is this: One of you says, 'I follow Paul'; another, 'I follow Apollos'; another, 'I follow Cephas'; still another, 'I follow Christ'"* (1 Cor. 1:12). This is a classic account of one of the major problems for the Church throughout all times—to divide itself and follow certain leaders or certain systems and create groups apart from others. This is pure and simple disunity which weakens and paralyzes the Body. Jesus said: *"If a kingdom is divided against itself, that kingdom cannot stand "* (Mark 3:24). He did not exclude the Kingdom of God in this statement. Division is the main reason why the Church so many times has been down on its knees—not in powerful prayer and intercession—but fallen and oppressed by its enemies simply because it couldn't stand anymore.

Paul uses the names of three men in this teaching—*including his own*—as potential instruments of division. This brings an important point to light. Any leader, even if he is largely "right" and "good," can contribute to division if there is wrongful attention put on him. This must be clearly understood both by the shepherds as well as the flock. The fourth example used by Paul are those that say they follow Christ. In other words, they would have nothing to do with leadership by Paul or others. This may sound quite spiritual—to follow Christ only. But in the context of spiritual leadership, it is simply a rejection of the way in which Christ has elected to exercise His authority in the Body. They supposedly want to follow Christ, but refuse to acknowledge those whom the Lord has chosen to carry out His leadership in the Church. These are people that are simply rejecting spiritual authority and are out there on their own, just as divided from the Body as anyone who would be wrongfully focused on man.

Paul then asks a simple question: *"Is Christ divided?"* If we act like the Corinthians did here, we must believe that Christ is in fact divided. On the other hand, if we understand that Christ is not divided and that the Body truly is one, we must steer away from the attention on man and the parties created within the Church by this attitude. Later, Paul uses Apollos and himself as examples that the Corinthians may learn to no longer act as if Christ was divided. *"Brothers, for your sake I have applied this to myself and Apollos, so that through our example you would learn the meaning of: 'Keep in line with the Scripture,' and do not boast about one man at the expense of another"* (1 Cor. 4:6, paraphrased by author from Swedish Bible version). This effectively teaches us that any celebrity mentality, VIP status, Who's Who ranking, popularity contest, award ceremony, or any other action that would promote attention on man and produce favoritism among leadership, does not belong in the Church. It might create certain excitement in the visible realm, but will only create division in the spiritual realm. This is quite a subtle area where Satan has been able to greatly infiltrate the Church. If he can divide the Body in this way, he has severely crippled its ability to stand up and fight. This is what has happened through the attention-on-man syndrome, which is a direct threat to real oneness among Christians.

There is a strong yearning in the heart of the Lord for true unity among His people, as expressed in His own prayer in John 17. Spiritual unity in the Body of Christ really does not require some "super" revelation. But it does require that we turn our eyes off man and on to Christ. Then oneness in the church will come naturally and the Body will be made whole.

~Chapter 5~
IN HIS NAME

Matthew 18:20

Jesus gave a significant promise which has been greatly cherished by the Church throughout history. *"For where two or three are gathered in My name, there am I in the midst of them"* (Matt. 18:20 KJV). This well-known verse has been quoted for all kinds of reasons—from truly understanding His presence to the attempt to put the best face on low attendance in Sunday night services. It gives however, great assurance that although we cannot see and hear Him like a human being, His presence is real and He is participating with us in a powerful way. This has always been a source of great encouragement for the Church.

Let us try to understand more clearly the conditions under which this promise will be in effect. Jesus said that we had to be gathered *in His name*. Other circumstances are not important. The physical place is not important. It can be a church, a home, in the woods, on the beach, in a restaurant, in an office, in a factory, or even on the moon (!), which has become an interesting new possibility for this promise in our days. Remember that God does not live in temples made by man. He lives by His Spirit in the temple of our bodies. Sometimes the Church is deceived into thinking that a certain church or other building, a certain place where God moved strongly in the past, or a place where God mightily used one of His servants before would better ensure His presence. So we think that we should really go there to be close to God. There is nothing wrong with physical facilities and suitable places to meet. But let's not get confused and make this a prerequisite for the Lord's presence.

The style and form of our meeting is not important either. Let us never think that there is something sacred in our outward traditions, whether these are based on strict fundamental thinking or "free" charismatic behavior, or anything else in between. Frankly, there can be just as much tradition in certain of the so-called informal movements who have gotten stuck in the bondage of having to constantly prove through their actions that they are truly "free." Christianity is never form, style, or tradition. It is life, and life is free and expresses itself in many ways. If we limit the presence of God to certain style and tradition, we will greatly hinder the dynamics of the Kingdom of God. And if we maintain that God could not possibly be present with certain others because they don't do things like we do, we are sadly mistaken. God does not look for outside systems, forms, and traditions. He looks for hearts that are willing to yield to Him.

The only condition that must be fulfilled for Christ to be present is that we are gathered in His name. It is not enough that He lives within each of us individually. When we gather, it appears that there has to be some kind of mutual agreement and invitation in order for Him to actively participate. What does it mean to be gathered in His name? Is it simply a phrase to be used as a headline for Christian activities? Is it a sentence established to create an appropriate ending to our prayers: "In Jesus' Name, Amen"? No, it has to do with our deepest reason and motive for gathering. To truly gather in His name must mean that He has actually called us together. We have come for His sake—nothing else. This does not happen simply because we quote a phrase from the Bible. It can only be the case if our hearts have embraced the reality of this truth. Then Jesus is the very reason for our gathering and the promise of His presence is in effect.

Is it possible that many times, although we quote this scripture with fervor, we are totally outside its reality? Is it possible that because of the way we often use man's name in God's work, we place ourselves in a position which is contradictory to the conditions under which this promise is in effect? Do we have to go so far as to conclude that Jesus might not be actively present at all (other than His omnipresence as part of the Godhead) in some gatherings, even though they carry the headline of being done in His name? Since Jesus said that we are to be gathered in His name, it also means that we are *not* to be gathered in any other name. Or seemingly be gathered in His name *because* of any other name. If we assemble in or because of other names, we are really not together in His name and have in essence stripped Jesus of His Lordship and prominence. This raises an interesting question. We know that Jesus is in the midst where two or three believers are truly gathered in His name. But what happens when two or three thousand Christians are assembled—officially in the name of Jesus—but really where some interesting names among His servants were used to get the crowds in? Perhaps even the names of those who have gained prominence because of their previous (or current!) work for the enemy!

These issues are very important with regard to the Church's right to claim the promise of the Lord's presence. In our eagerness to hold successful gatherings as far as numbers and statistics, we so often fall right into the attention-on-man syndrome. We might create big things and apparent success for the moment, not realizing that at the same time we have driven Christ right out from our midst, thereby suppressing spiritual fruit that will last. We have effectively cancelled out the promise which was intended to be the very strength of our gathering. In fact, the Holy Spirit is grieved when we, under the heading of doing things in the name of Jesus, still put so much focus and attention on the role of man. It would almost be better that we did not involve the Lord at all and called things by their correct name: Entertainment, performance, show, or whatever else displays man's abilities. God is not interested in letting His name be used by us to do our thing. Instead, He wants to use us to do His thing.

But isn't the Lord present where His word is read, spoken, and sung? And didn't even Paul indicate that it's okay to preach *"in every way,"* even out of selfish ambition? *"But what does it matter? The important thing is that in every way, whether from false motives or true, Christ is preached"* (Phil. 1:18). Yes, the Lord will reach out with the gospel of salvation in all kinds of ways. Even through situations where the motives might be completely off-base. But this is not a license for the church to continue in pride and wrongful focus on man. And it appears that Paul in this case is not endorsing wrong motives but rather takes the "high road" in the situation so that he would not fall into the same trap of competition as the men he is talking about. In order for the fullness of the Lord's presence to be a reality among His people, we must prioritize His name. The base for the promise is clear: In His Name. Not in somebody else's or for some other reason. The motive behind our gatherings is extremely important.

It is therefore imperative for the Church to teach—in words and in deed—the correct priority order of attention. Christians will not truly learn that Christ is the center, if we by word teach that all glory and attention must go to Him, but at the same time in practical reality put great focus and attention on man within the Church. We must not create a distorted picture of Christ by lifting up man incorrectly in His work. We must not tempt people to gather in other names than His. We must not so desire to see big crowds that we no longer can gather in His name alone. Let's separate ourselves from the attitude of this world and turn away from the attention-on-man syndrome, or we may lose the very presence of the Lord Himself.

There is also another most important aspect involved here. Hebrews states: *"The Son is the radiance of God's glory and the exact representation of His being, sustaining all things by His powerful word. After He had provided purification for sins, He sat down at the right hand of the Majesty in heaven. So He became as much superior to the angels as the name He has inherited is superior to theirs"* (Heb. 1:3–4). Jesus' work on earth, bringing superiority to His name, is the very reflection of God and His glory. The Father gave the only begotten Son, and the Son obediently fulfilled His mission on earth. This will be the object of eternal praise in heaven. *"After this I looked and there before me was a great multitude that no one could count, from every nation, tribe, people and language, standing before the throne and in front of the Lamb. They were wearing white robes and were holding palm branches in their hands. And they cried out in a loud voice: 'Salvation belongs to our God, who sits on the throne, and to the Lamb'"* (Rev. 7:9–10). Christ, the Lamb, is always the center of heaven's worship and praise. It is therefore quite a serious thing to wrongfully involve man's name in God's work on earth, which is also totally based on the glory and power of Christ. Frankly, it is almost like a slap in the face of the Almighty to put any importance on man's name and position — whether our own or others' — serving in the Church. Man can only participate as a recipient of His grace and mercy. Full attention and glory must go to the One who already has gained full attention in the view of the Father: Jesus Christ, the Son of Man. *"To Him who sits on the throne and to the Lamb be praise and honor and glory and power forever and ever!"* (Rev. 5:13).

Event Christianity and Goosebumps Addiction

It is interesting to note the size of gathering Jesus used when He gave us the promise of His presence: Two or three. We know that Jesus lives within each individual Christian and is with us always. And when He assures us of His special presence in meetings with several believers, He uses the lowest possible numbers next to one: *two or three.* Note also that He did not say that the more of us that are gathered, the stronger His presence and power will be. Two or three truly gathered in His name is quite enough for Him to be present in all His fullness.

This highlights an attitude which sometimes impacts the Church quite negatively: The search for Event Christianity. Many Christians live under the illusion that the bigger the event, the larger the auditorium, the more numerous the crowd—God's presence will then be greater and His work more powerful. We should immediately say that there is nothing wrong with large gatherings and big meetings. God can certainly speak through these as well. But the danger is this. In order to create the big events, we find that we many times have to use big names, celebrities, and secular entertainment style PR in order to make them successful. We thereby are in great danger of falling right into the attention-on-man syndrome. This does not apply only to the super events that the church has become more and more accustomed to. There are also many local churches who try to make every Sunday an event so that people would feel good about coming.

The measuring stick of the perceived success of an event—whether small, medium, large, or extra large—seems to always be numbers. How large an auditorium? How many in attendance? How many went forward? How much money was raised, etc.? Ask just about any Christian regarding the success of a certain gathering and he will answer you with numbers. And so important have these kind of measurements become to the Church, that we are more and more confused regarding the true presence of Jesus versus the outward greatness of the event. Not only that. Sometimes like drug addicts, we get so hooked on Event Christianity that we constantly chase after bigger and better gatherings so that we may experience an even "higher" blessing. We do not understand that when doing so, we might simply be emotionally charged by our focus on man and not necessarily in the true presence of Christ. This is why it is so important to really understand what Jesus was saying when He gave this promise. Two or three — the most un-eventful gathering — is enough for the fullness of His presence. And Jesus did not say that one had to be a speaker, the other a singer, and the third a listener. Two or three "grassroot-Christians" are enough for the fullness of His ministry to be revealed.

There is also another side to this which requires caution. We could call it "Goosebumps Addiction." The attraction of the event often produces an emotional high on a level of the soul, not necessarily the spirit. To walk into a packed-out auditorium gives all of us a good feeling. But it may have nothing to do with a spiritual work. The large crowds may simply be a result of some hot names and shrewd advertising. But it gives us a good feeling anyway. And when we hear top singers superbly present the Scriptures and Christian thoughts in high notes, accompanied by kabooming drums and super-charged synthesizers, we get goosebumps. And this is not bad. As long as we don't confuse it with what is really happening on the spiritual level. The celebrity speaker delivers the message eloquently with intelligence, humor, emotions, etc., and we are all touched. There is nothing wrong with that either. Praise God for those who have the ability to effectively address the crowds. But we must not become mesmerized by the outward wrapping around God's message, like children who can endlessly stare at the colorful wrapping around Christmas presents. Many Christians have become so addicted to the attention on man, wrapped in event/goosebumps Christianity, that they almost forget where the real strength of the Church is: Two or three (or more) gathered in *His* name.

The great event has already happened. Two thousand years ago on Calvary's cross. The world does not need any other event — ever. We repeat, there is absolutely nothing wrong with large Christian gatherings led by effective communicators. But we must always make sure that the event happens around Jesus, His name, and finished work. Not around the abilities and talents of the messengers God might use at the moment. No amount of Scripture quotes, powerful teaching, and beautiful worship music can bring back the Lord's presence unless the primary condition is fulfilled: That we are truly gathered in *His* name.

Let's look at this also from a little different perspective using electronics as an illustration. Any kind of electronic sound device such as a radio, stereo system, or tape recorder is made up of a complex array of electronic components and circuitry in order to bring speech or music to our ears. However, the last component in line must be a loudspeaker so that the electronic signal can be translated into sounds which can be received by human ears. All the work of the electronic circuitry would be of no use unless there is a final loudspeaker which can bring it to our understanding. In a typical low-cost, portable transistor radio, the speaker is a very simple and cheap component. Maybe a dollar or two. When you turn on your tabletop radio, you are suddenly in contact with all sorts of activity. The music you hear has been produced with sophisticated sound equipment by skillful musicians and singers. The radio voice speaks into high quality microphones and the electronic signal passes through expensive transmitters in order to reach your home. But the loudspeaker in your radio, even if it is a small, one dollar speaker, is completely essential to make all this available to you. The loudspeaker can never boast of having made the music or created the radio speech. But it just happens to be an absolute necessity to connect you with those who in fact have produced the message carried by the electronic signal.

There is great emphasis today on the quality of electronically reproduced sound for our listening pleasure. Some have state-of-the-art stereo systems costing thousands of dollars, where the speakers alone might cost several hundred dollars. The music played through a hi-fi system will of course sound much more pleasant than the same music heard through a tabletop radio. However, let's say there is a warning of severe weather conditions

transmitted over the airwaves. The person who hears this announce-
ment through a radio with a low-cost speaker will get the message
just as loud and clear as the one who hears it through his expensive
hi-fi speakers. At that point, nobody will be concerned with the
quality of the sound, but rather focus on the reality of the message.
The person who heard the message through his big hi-fi system
will not be more alert to the pending emergency than the one
who listened through his little tabletop radio with telephone-like
sound quality. In fact, it's very possible that the man with the expensive stereo equipment would leave his comfortable recliner,
turn off his hi-fi system, and look for a simple, portable radio in
order to stay informed and start to prepare for whatever needs to
be done based on the message he had just heard. He would no
longer be driven by the quality and pleasure resulting from his
sophisticated sound system, but rather by the reality of the message that was transmitted.

This is similar to the spiritual realm. God has a complex set of
components and circuitry, and is continually transmitting spiritual signals to mankind. He has produced programs, if you will,
that are always on the air and ready for immediate reception. In
His divine plan, God has placed man as a loudspeaker at the end
of this circuitry in order to bring His signals to the world. Man is
not to produce anything in himself, only communicate that which
has already been produced and transmitted through God's spiritual circuitry. Most of us are like small one dollar speakers, while
some may resemble the fuller and greater sound of expensive hi-fi
systems. But in either case, it is almost silly to focus on the speaker
which is absolutely nothing in itself unless someone greater transmitted a signal through it.

Sometimes our Christian gatherings look more like exhibitions
where we get together to enjoy loud-speakers and evaluate their
ability to create goosebumps due to their great hi-fi qualities. It is
no secret that the Christian community spends hundreds of mil-
lions of dollars yearly to enjoy special events, hear messages, and

receive ministry which the Lord could provide just as easily in settings where only two, three or just a few are gathered. And sometimes we might even miss the message from the Producer Himself in these events, because we concentrate so much on the loudspeakers. When we truly wake up to the reality of the message and understand who speaks it, the loudspeaker at the end of the circuitry becomes less and less significant.

Kingdom Territory

Like any other kingdom, the Kingdom of God has certain borders within which it is contained. It occupies a specific territory in the spiritual realm where Kingdom laws and Kingdom principles are in effect. This is in essence the area within which God is working. The Kingdom of God is at the very heart of God's plan of redemption. The gospel of the Kingdom was the main theme for Jesus' ministry on earth. It is therefore important for every Christian to understand that unless we have positioned ourselves on Kingdom territory, we cannot apply Kingdom principles or count on God's promises to be in effect. Even if we seemingly venture far into enemy territory in the spiritual battle, we must (and have the right to) bring a piece of the Kingdom of God with us. Thus, we can still stand on Kingdom territory while facing the enemy, much like an embassy on foreign soil. This was effectively displayed when Jesus after His death on the cross brought the newly established Kingdom of God with Him into the regions of darkness and took the keys of death from Satan. Right before Christ's death, the repentant robber crucified with Him, said: "'Jesus, remember me when You come into Your Kingdom.' Jesus answered him, 'I tell you the truth, today you will be with Me in paradise'" (Luke 23:42–43). Jesus entered death with new authority based on a new Kingdom with new laws. Satan himself was forced to turn over the keys and Kingdom authority was fully displayed in the chambers of darkness. And that same day the first citizen of the heavenly Kingdom had his name confirmed in the Lamb's Book of Life. Every Christian is now entitled to walk in the footsteps of Jesus, with Kingdom authority. *"And I confer on you a Kingdom, just as My Father conferred one on Me . . ."* (Luke 22: 29).

However, this will only work if we move on Kingdom territory. Otherwise we will only fool ourselves and others. God's promises and principles are not magic formulas that can be spoken over any situation as a quick antidote against sin and evil. They are to be applied on the territory for which they were established, just like laws for earthly kingdoms and territories. For example, to claim your rights as an American is only good if you do it on American territory. Not only does it not work to claim American rights in many other countries, it may also make the situation worse. If you assert your American status there, you could be treated even more harshly because of that. It works the same way in the spiritual realm. Do not for a minute think that you can wander into the territory of darkness and when things get hot start to claim Kingdom rights. Kingdom laws apply to Kingdom territory.

Since this is the case, it is extremely important to understand the borders of the Kingdom and the geography of its territories. The definition of Kingdom territory and its borders could be looked upon from many angles. However, one short verse in Colossians gives us a good summary: *"And whatever you do, whether in word or deed, do it all in the name of the Lord Jesus, giving thanks to God the Father through Him"* (Col. 3:17). In a sense, this is all the definition we need of the borders of the Kingdom of God. To do everything in word and actions in the name of Jesus, which then ensures that God's will is carried out, thus bringing thanks and praise to God. When we do this — we are on Kingdom territory. When we don't — we're not. This is a simple but accurate "geography" lesson.

Remember however, what we have already discussed. To do everything in the name of Jesus does not mean to simply use the phrase "In Jesus' name" as a magic formula to headline our gatherings or end our prayers and speeches, thereby releasing God's mystical power. It means to lift Jesus up to His rightful position; the King, the Head, the Ruler, the Centerpoint, the One who deserves total attention. And when we do so, the focus must steer away from man. The light and glory of the risen King is so great, that to even think of placing focus on any man should be out of the question. Even if the stage is filled with so-called big names and VIPs in a Christian event, when Jesus steps on the scene (which He does if we are truly gathered in His name) all human beings basically end up on the same level compared to Him. If a millionaire steps in to a room, it really doesn't matter if some of the others have ten dollars and some have one hundred dollars in their bank accounts. Compared to the millionaire, they are all basically on the same level anyway. When Jesus is given this kind of attention and position in the Church, Kingdom authority and power will be at work. This is the reason why we should never unduly focus on man, only see man as a servant and instrument in the hands of Him who deserves all glory and attention.

This also involves our protection as individual Christians and the protection for the Church collectively. The Scripture states: *"The name of the Lord is a strong tower; the righteous run to it and are safe"* (Prov. 18:10). A tower was the symbol of defense and protection in old times. It was a place for early detection of enemy attacks and effective defense and shelter against such attacks. The name of the Lord is still our *"strong tower"* in defense against the enemy. But only when we truly proceed in the name of the Lord are we sheltered from Satan's attacks. We then run to the *"strong tower"* of Jesus' name and *"are safe."* The expression "are safe" in this Scripture passage literally means "are set on high." This could be compared to another well-known and much appreciated Scripture. *"And God raised us up with Christ and seated us with Him in the heavenly realms in Christ Jesus . . ."* (Eph. 2:6). However, if we through the influence of the attention-on-man syndrome downgrade our ability to focus on the name of the Lord alone, we are lowered to a less than "strong tower" position. We are then not only unable to break forward with God's Kingdom to rescue others from enemy territory, but also quite vulnerable to enemy attack right where we stand.

God spoke through Isaiah about the oppression of His people. *"At first My people went down to Egypt to live; lately, Assyria has oppressed them. 'And now what do I have here?' declares the Lord. 'For My people have been taken away for nothing, and those who rule them mock,' declares the Lord. 'And all day long My name is constantly blasphemed. Therefore My people will know My name; therefore in that day they will know that it is I who foretold it. Yes, it is I'"* (Isa. 52:4–6). What is God's answer for oppression and attack against His people? It is that His people would know His name. To know the name—the depth and character—of Him whose glory and power surpasses anyone else and makes every enemy flee. On the other hand, to not know His name, or not correctly prioritize His name, assures us of problems and oppression. It invites the enemy and we hopelessly look to the names of man, our own or others', for strength and victory.

The time has come for the Church to deeply seek the name of the Lord and to receive revelation knowledge of who He really is. The Almighty speaks to His people now as in days past: *"Therefore My people will know My name."* Victory and freedom from oppression will come when the Lord's name is correctly prioritized and declared among His people. The glory of the Lord always appears under the banner of His name. This also means that every other name—no matter whose it is—must fade away in the background.

Another way to understand and define the borders of Kingdom territory would be by what we could call the earthquake method, i.e., to observe the intensity and amount of shaking going on in the Church. From time to time, God allows certain things to occur which greatly shake the Christian community on a local, national or international basis. These are never pleasant times, but nevertheless they happen. We often blame the devil for these "unfair" attacks, and he is certainly the one who does the attacking. But we must also understand that he has the right to do so for now, since this takes place on his territory. Let us explain. A well-known Scripture states: *"Therefore, since we are receiving a Kingdom that cannot be shaken, let us be thankful, and so worship God acceptably with reverence and awe, for our God is a consuming fire"* (Heb. 12:28–29). God's Kingdom cannot be shaken by anyone or anything. Not by man, not by angels, not by powers of darkness, not by circumstances even though they might seem overwhelming to man. His Kingdom stands firm through all ages and all circumstances. However, that which is not placed on Kingdom territory can and will be shaken. This is what takes place in situations of great shaking within the Church. The enemy finds areas which are connected to his territory and he shakes them vigorously. Frankly, this has to happen as part of God's plan to define and refine His Kingdom among us.

When we understand how to place ourselves solely on Kingdom territory, we cannot be shaken. However, when we compromise the borders of the Kingdom and place our feet on "foreign" soil, we then become open to a possible severe earthquake treatment. And it is obvious that many things within the Church, built around man's name according to the attention-on-man syndrome, are allowed to be shaken since this syndrome is outside Kingdom borders. Such shaking will likely increase more and more as the Spirit of the Lord directs God's people away from enemy territory, in order for the Church to position itself completely inside the Kingdom that cannot be shaken.

We find an interesting account regarding Kingdom territory when Jesus teaches about the greatest commandment. A theologian had heard a discussion between Jesus and the Sadducees regarding marriage at the resurrection of the dead. *"One of the teachers of the law came and heard them debating. Noticing that*

*Jesus had given them a good answer, he asked Him, 'Of all the com-
mandments, which is the most important?' 'The most important one,'
answered Jesus, 'is this: "Hear, O Israel, the Lord our God, the Lord
is one. Love the Lord your God with all your heart and with all your
soul and with all your mind and with all your strength." The second
is this: "Love your neighbor as yourself." There is no commandment
greater than these.' 'Well said, teacher,' the man replied. 'You are
right in saying that God is one and there is no other but Him. To
love Him with all your heart, with all your understanding and with
all your strength, and to love your neighbor as yourself is more important than all burnt offerings and sacrifices.' When Jesus saw that he
had answered wisely, He said to him, 'You are not far from the Kingdom of God'"* (Mark 12:28–34).

Jesus gives us here a clear understanding of our relationship
to God as well as our relationship to other human beings. He
also gives us an understanding regarding the territory of the Kingdom of God, indicating the existence of spiritual "distance" by
the fact that human beings can be closer or farther away from its
borders. First, Jesus uses an expression which was very important to the Old Covenant Israelites: *"Hear, O Israel, the Lord our
God, the Lord is one."* This expresses the important understanding that there is only one God and that there are to be no idols
beside Him. Further, we are to love the Lord with all our heart,
soul, mind, and strength. In other words, to the ultimate extent.
Then Jesus quotes the second greatest commandment: *"Love your
neighbor as yourself."*

Included in this teaching are two very important principles
which define the borders of the Kingdom. First, love the Lord
more than anything else. Put Him in the highest place. Focus on
Him and make sure that nothing else even comes close to com-
peting with His position. Deny yourself in order to follow Him.
Indeed, love Him more than your own life. This is the essence of
Christianity. To love the Lord because He first loved us. To be
totally consumed with Him. To die to ourselves that He might

live in and through us. To set our heart, soul, mind, and strength totally on Him. The second principle is this: Love your neighbor as yourself. Notice carefully the difference here. We are to love the Lord above everything else, even our own life. But we are to love other human beings in the same way that we love ourselves. In other words, we are to see the Lord as high and lifted up above anyone and anything else. But our view of man should be that everyone is on the same level.

This is an important spiritual principle that establishes Kingdom territory. Love your neighbor as yourself—no more, no less. The teacher of the law, whom Jesus was talking to, understood all this theologically and intellectually. And Jesus said about Him: *"You are not far from the Kingdom of God."* His problem was of course, (as has always been the case with human beings), to not just understand God's word, but to live it. Especially since the commandment to love the Lord would now have to include the understanding and acceptance of Jesus as the Christ.

Again, Kingdom territory is clearly defined here. The Lord is high above everything else. All men are on an equal level below. God has no favorites, no children that are more important than others. There is no royalty presiding over others in God's Kingdom, apart from the fact that we are all a royal priesthood. There are no VIPs or stars in the Church apart from the Very Important Prince of Peace and the bright Morning Star Himself. Any other understanding and application will put us outside Kingdom territory and place us in great danger of being injured or killed by enemy fire.

When Jesus expresses His grief over Jerusalem and its rejection of Him, He makes the following statement: *"I tell you, you will not see Me again until you say, 'Blessed is He who comes in the name of the Lord'"* (Luke 13:35). This is mainly a prophecy pointing to the time in the future when Israel will finally discover Jesus as their Messiah. But remember also that Jesus said to His disciples: *"I will not leave you as orphans; I will come to you. Before long, the world*

*will not see Me anymore, but you will see Me. . . . All this I have
spoken while still with you. But the Counselor, the Holy Spirit, whom
the Father will send in My name, will teach you all things and will
remind you of everything I have said to you"* (John 14:18–19, 25–26).

Jesus is already back for His disciples and they see Him through
the revelation of the Holy Spirit in their hearts. Blessed is He who
comes, the Holy Spirit, in the name of the Lord. Jesus said that
the Father would send the Spirit *"in My name."* Again we see the
borders of the Kingdom. The Holy Spirit operates in Jesus' name,
not in His own name or any other's. And when the Holy Spirit
calls, equips, and uses a human being for service in the Kingdom
of God, it will be done in exactly the same way: In the name of
Jesus. Not in the person's own name, the name of an organization,
or any other human entity. Remember, that to do everything in
the name of the Lord, in word and in deed, means that He takes
absolute control, attention, and glory. Blessed is he/she, man or
woman on earth, who proceeds in such a manner in service for
the Kingdom. Frankly, there is no blessing otherwise. It has to be
done this way. When man's name is unduly inserted into the picture, it may seemingly have a positive effect in the form of greater
audiences, etc. But when we carefully examine the situation, the
forces at work may be mainly the result of PR schemes, marketing
strategies, entertainment attitudes, and perhaps pure idolatry. God
will not add His blessing to this.

Once when asked by the Pharisees how the Kingdom of God
could be observed, Jesus answered that it would not be seen as a
regular kingdom with visible borders since *"the Kingdom of God
is within you"* (Luke 17:21). Thus, the only visible expression of
God's Kingdom in the world is through those who have bowed
down to and are continuously proceeding in the name of the
Lord. Their inward man—being the soil of the Kingdom—and
their outward attitude of doing everything, whether in word or
deed, in the name of the Lord, is the sole expression of this Kingdom on earth. God has no other way to display His name and to

announce the completed work of redemption through His Son. It has to be done through the inward Kingdom and the outward proclamation of the Lord's name by those who have made themselves subject to His will. A Church proceeding with religious motions, "Christian" activities, good and moral principles—but not truly in the name of the Lord—really has little to do with the Kingdom of God. Only when we proceed in His name, and in His name alone, are we on Kingdom territory.

The final manifestation of this is described in Philippians 2. "*. . . that at the name of Jesus every knee should bow, in heaven and on earth and under the earth, and every tongue confess that Jesus Christ is Lord, to the glory of God the Father*" (Phil. 2:10–11). All mankind will finally acknowledge the Kingdom of God by confessing the name and Lordship of Christ to the glory of God the Father. Some with great joy, since this is familiar territory and simply the ultimate opportunity to once again lift up the name of the Lord. Others, greatly surprised and compelled to confess Christ's Lordship before being eternally separated from God. It is a remarkable thought that all human beings will come in His name, having understood that all other names are nothing. This time the beauty and holiness of the Kingdom of God will shine like never before.

God's Character

When God appears to Moses in the burning bush and instructs him to go back to Egypt to lead the Israelites out of bondage, a prophetic act foretelling the work of Christ, Moses asks: "*"Suppose I go to the Israelites and say to them, "The God of your fathers has sent me to you," and they ask me, "What is His name?" Then what shall I tell them?' God said to Moses, 'I am who I am. This is what you are to say to the Israelites: I AM has sent me to you'*" (Exod. 3:13–14). The answer God gives provides Moses not only with a name to bring to the Israelites but also an understanding of the very character of God. Many sermons have been preached on the great power, provision, and faithfulness of the mighty I AM who revealed Himself to Moses that day. God is very particular in this respect. He desires that when we call upon His name, we not only identify a certain divine entity somewhere out there, but that we understand the character and the heart of the One we are calling on.

This is most certainly the case in the New Covenant as well. God has elected to reveal His name, His character, His principles, His grace, and His power through the work of His Son. *"And I have declared unto them Thy name, and will declare it: that the love wherewith Thou hast loved Me may be in them, and I in them"* (John 17:26 KJV). The Body of Christ on earth is God's "I AM" to the world in New Covenant time. It is the Kingdom displaying God's character among mankind. We repeat, Jesus said: *"My Kingdom is within you,"* thus stating that this is a Kingdom expressed by inward character. We Christians do not walk around with swords, guns, and documents of human authority to force the eternal God upon others. But we are supposed to proceed in the power and authority of love, joy, peace, patience, etc., which displays the mind of Christ—the very character of the Kingdom. This is why we are baptized in the name of Jesus, confirming our death and resurrection with Him into this new state of mind and spirit. *"For in Christ all the fullness of the Deity lives in bodily form, and you have been given fullness in Christ, . . . having been buried with Him in baptism and raised with Him through your faith in the power of God, who raised Him from the dead"* (Col. 2:9–12). The fullness and character of God becomes ours because of Jesus and we confirm this by baptism in His name. *"You are all sons of God through faith in Christ Jesus, for all of you who were baptized into Christ have clothed yourselves with Christ"* (Gal. 3:26–27). We are not to consider any man's name or action as part of this work. Paul found it necessary to make this clear to the Corinthians in response to their quarrels and division: *"Is Christ divided? Was Paul crucified for you? Were you baptized into the name of Paul?"* (1 Cor. 1:13). Man's role is only to direct others to Christ and baptize them into His name, not the names of God's servants or religious organizations. When we rise from the baptism, we confirm that we have clothed ourselves with Christ, His fullness, His character and His life. Not that we have pledged loyalty to certain human beings or their works.

Considering that the name of the Lord is not only used to identify the most powerful entity in the universe but also to display His very character, we must think of the following as well. When we unduly introduce man's name into God's work, we begin to distort the view of His character. The attention-on-man syndrome has the effect of inappropriately introducing perceived aspects of God's nature which really are not His. Only when we are fully clothed with Christ can the nature of God be seen. When we break out of this cover by wrongfully introducing our own or other people's name into His work, (and thus human character traits), shadows will start to fall on the very name of God. Even the most "powerful" names in Christianity are not good enough. Man is man and God is God. If we focus on man, we will reap from the flesh. If we focus on the Lord, we will reap from the Spirit.

This is particularly important with regard to new Christians. It sometimes appears that we introduce people to God with the help of the names, characters, and abilities of certain men and women. This is very dangerous because from time to time these will fail also. Only Christ is perfect and will never fail. Only His name should be our guiding light. The saying is true that the only Bible many sinners will ever read will be the lives of Christians. But let's make sure that it is His book that they read in our lives, and not our's or that of VIPs or celebrities. We must not place man in the picture in such a way that he receives the focus, since the attention-on-man syndrome effectively hinders God to display His character. This syndrome fools the world and confuses the Church as to who God truly is.

The Mind of Christ

As already discussed, God's character is displayed in New Testament time through the mind of Christ within the Church and its individual members. Paul states: *"But we have the mind of Christ"* (1 Cor. 2:16). What is the mind of Christ and how does it apply to the individual Christian and the Church collectively? How can it truly be said of us that we have the mind of Christ? This foundational truth can only be received and understood by faith through the revelation of the Holy Spirit. It is He who applies the work of Christ in our lives and leads us forward in spiritual growth and holiness. The more we understand and receive the mind of Christ through this powerful work of the Spirit, the more we grow into spiritual maturity. Maturity is always a matter of mindset. In natural life, someone can be big and strong when it comes to bones and muscles. However, if that person has a childish mindset, he is considered immature anyway. This is also very much true in the spiritual realm. Someone might be able to quote Scriptures left and right, be very active in church work and perform all kinds of religious duties. But unless all this is done with the mind of Christ, he would still have to be considered an immature Christian.

This is one of God's great problems today. He has too many children and too few grown-ups, as seen from the perspective of spiritual maturity. Many take the promises and principles of God's word and try to apply them with a mind that is influenced by this world's attitude and not renewed by the mind of Christ. Therefore the Church often looks like a playground with games of pretending, rather than a place where the real thing happens by the actions of mature Christians.

We find a most helpful teaching in Philippians in our quest to understand the mind of Christ. *"Let this mind be in you, which was also in Christ Jesus"* (Phil. 2:5 KJV). Or, as translated in the NIV: *"Your attitude should be the same as that of Christ Jesus."* The verses which follow are a very powerful summary of Jesus' mindset and attitude. This attitude made Him a totally useful instrument in God's plan of salvation. It made Him become the One in front of whom every knee will bow and every tongue confess in the end. *"Who, being in the very nature God, did not consider equality with God something to be grasped, but made Himself nothing, taking the very nature of a servant, being made in human likeness. And being found in appearance as a man, He humbled Himself and became obedient to death — even death on the cross! Therefore God exalted Him to the highest place and gave Him the name that is above every name, that at the name of Jesus every knee should bow, in heaven and on earth and under the earth, and every tongue confess that Jesus Christ is Lord, to the glory of God the Father"* (Phil. 2:6–11). This familiar Scripture contains major characteristics of the mind and attitude of Christ which is the model for us. We will look specifically at three of these characteristics. Two are more easily understood, while the third one is less well-known but may be the very key to Jesus' service on earth.

First, humility. Verse 8 reads as follows in the Amplified Bible: *"And after He had appeared in human form, He abased and humbled Himself [still further] . . ."* To abase oneself means to lower in rank, office, prestige, or esteem. This is a much important part of the mindset that we are to have also. Remember that the Church is not a place to gain prestige and esteem. It is a place to lose it!

Secondly, obedience. Jesus submitted completely to God's authority and command — not His own will. It is interesting to note, that Jesus in His life on earth had to learn obedience. He came from a situation with His Father where there simply was no disobedience. Thus, no one had to learn obedience. But as the Son of Man He was tempted to disobey like us and therefore had to learn obedience to His Father. *"During the days of Jesus' life on earth, He offered up prayers and petitions with loud cries and tears to the One who could save Him from death, and*

He was heard because of his reverent submission. Although He was a Son, He learned obedience from what He suffered, and once made perfect, He became the source of eternal salvation for all who obey Him and was designated by God to be High Priest, in the order of Melchizedek" (Heb. 5:7–10). Most Christians understand the importance of obedience. No work of God can be accomplished unless there is obedience as displayed in the mindset and attitude of Christ.

Much has been taught regarding humility and obedience. But the third characteristic has not received quite the same exposure. However, this characteristic may well be the very centerpoint of the mind of Christ, the very base on which God could use His Son on earth and break the enemy's back through Him. Verse 7: *". . . but made Himself nothing."* It is quite interesting to see the variety of translations of this statement in different versions. NIV: *"But made Himself nothing."* KJV: *"But made Himself of no reputation."* Amplified: *"But stripped Himself [of all privileges and rightful dignity]."* Living Bible: *"But laid aside His mighty power and glory."* NAS: *". . . but emptied Himself."* These statements could be summarized in one word: Nothingness. This is the very backbone of the mind of Christ. He was willing to become "nothing" for the Father. To let go of His reputation. To empty Himself. To lay aside power and glory. To strip Himself of privileges and dignity—even that which was rightfully His. To become nothing so that the Father could become everything in Him. This is an extremely important lesson for the Church in light of the attention-on-man syndrome. Who is willing to become "nothing" for the Lord? There are certainly many who are more than willing to become "something" for Him! Preferably "something big" which is talked about and celebrated by others. And who is willing to receive God's word from those who are "nothing"? The crowds are certainly more eager to gather for ministry from those who have a name and are "something" in the Church.

The "nothingness" of Christ is lacking substantially among God's people today. The Church is often boastful and prides itself on being "something" for God. But without the "nothingness" of Christ, there really is no true humility, true obedience, true authority, true power, and true ministry. Indeed, the very lack of spiritual "nothingness" reduces the Church to nothing, (i.e. being paralyzed, weak, etc.), as far as spiritual power and authority is concerned. Without the mind of Christ, who made Himself "nothing," there really is little opportunity for God to work.

This understanding is important for the Church collectively as well as the individual Christian. The Church is not a place to make a career and become "something." It is a place to achieve "nothingness." This is particularly important to teach new Christians. We must not mislead them into thinking that serving God is a career opportunity for personal advancement. Unfortunately, this frequently becomes their understanding when the attention-on-man syndrome is allowed to prevail. Neither is the Church a place to enjoy the fruit of those who have become "something" in the eyes of man. It is a place to receive blessings from Him who works best through those who are "nothing." We need a fresh and new revelation in this area both among the leadership as well as the flock.

Note carefully that this attitude was a willful act on Jesus' part. He made Himself nothing, He laid aside, He stripped Himself, etc. This is our model. Don't ask God to humble you or make you nothing. Sure, He can do that in an instant—with a force that will make your head spin. And sometimes He does. But He desires that we freely humble ourselves and make ourselves nothing, just like Jesus. This is what pleases the Lord. That we seek His ways and willingly follow them. Yes, we need the Holy Spirit to carry out all this in our lives. But the Spirit cannot work freely unless we willfully cooperate.

There is another lesson here as well. Jesus had a lifelong commitment to an attitude of "nothingness." We know very little about one of the most interesting parts of Jesus' ministry on earth, the time He spent with His disciples after the resurrection. *"After His suffer-ing, He showed Himself to these men and gave many convincing proofs that He was alive. He appeared to them over a period of forty days and spoke about the Kingdom of God"* (Acts 1:3). What a Bible school! To spend time with the risen Savior teaching about the Kingdom of God. Most likely this was the time when He put into perspective for His disciples what had happened and what it all meant. This made it possible for these men to later become mighty instruments in God's hand, some of them to write portions of the New Testament. However, Jesus also later showed that He could just as well use some-one who did not attend that magnificent Bible school. One example is Paul who wasn't even a believer at that time. Thank God for this or we would all have been at a disadvantage since we were not able to attend that school either.

One of the most spectacular features of this period however, was what Christ chose *not* to do. Remember that Jesus was con-stantly at odds with the Jewish priests and teachers. They hated Him since He did not fit their religious system and couldn't pos-sibly be the Messiah in their opinion. Finally, by enticing Judas to betray Him, by coming up with false accusations and by stir-ring up the crowds against Him, they succeeded in having Jesus killed by crucifixion. Just like they wanted it. However, after He rose from the dead, it would have taken Jesus no more than a few minutes to prove Himself and His resurrection. He could have gone to the Sanhedrin, stuck His head in the door and said: "Good morning! Nice day today!" This would no doubt have created the biggest headlines ever in the equivalent of the *Jerusalem Post* of those days, the *Mouth-to-Mouth Journal* or whatever carried the news.

What a victory this seemingly would have been! What a display of God's power! What a way to show these religious accusers and doubters for what they were! But the remarkable thing is that Jesus did not do this. Instead, the descendants from the religious leaders of those days still believe that Jesus is dead. They later heard reports from those who had seen the risen Savior but considered these as fantasies by religious fanatics. It is still the same today. The time has yet to come when Jesus will prove to all what really happened. However, the fact that Jesus did not show Himself alive to all the people was not a mistake in God's plan. The Apostle Peter makes an interesting statement to that effect when he speaks at the home of Cornelius: "... *God raised Him from the dead on the third day and caused Him to be seen. He was not seen by all the people, but by witnesses whom God had already chosen—by us who ate and drank with Him after He rose from the dead*" (Acts 10:40–41). It was God's deliberate plan that Jesus would be seen by just some, while the rest of us would have to find Him by their testimony and faith alone.

The point is this. The "nothingness" of Jesus' character extended to the other side of the resurrection as well. He did not have to prove anything or try to repair His reputation at that point. Not even with something as spiritual as His own resurrection from the dead! Jesus was fully satisfied to simply fulfill the will of the Father, whose plan was that the Son would be received by faith as the risen Savior in the hearts of men. Jesus spent forty days with those who were chosen by God, ready to understand and receive the secret wisdom of the Kingdom. But He had no need to prove Himself to anyone else, including the ones who from a human perspective needed the most to see Him alive. This is a remarkable lesson regarding the mind of Christ which we are to have also. In hardship and trials we are nothing, so there is really nothing to be defeated and we are free from the agony of trying to keep the flesh alive. In victory and flourishing ministry we are still nothing. So there is nothing to prove , no statistics to announce, no glory to be gained, no headlines to be established. All the glory goes to the Lord anyway.

Only if we have the mind of Christ will it be possible for God to bring us to the position where He really wants us. "*Therefore God exalted Him to the highest place and gave Him the name that is above every name*" (Phil. 2:9). Jesus' death on the cross was the primary reason why God exalted Him to a position of absolute authority and glory. But the cross would never have happened unless Jesus indeed had the mindset and attitude which we have discussed here. The same holds true for us. We can only reach the position God intends for us in His Kingdom if our attitude is the same as that of Christ Jesus. God can only fully use Christians with this mindset. They will not abuse the position God gives them or try to share the glory with the Lord, either for themselves or other human beings.

A *Church in Humility*

The true Church approaching the twenty-first century, which many believe could be the end-time Church, should be deeply characterized by the mind of Christ and must move in great humility. This is the only type of Church God can use as He proceeds to conclude this present age. This is why the Holy Spirit brings strong words of encouragement as well as rebuke and discipline to God's people. God has always used this two-fold approach—encouragement and rebuke—since He cannot build His work on an unclean foundation. When God called the prophet Jeremiah, He gave him clear instructions: "... *to uproot and tear down, to destroy and overthrow, to build and to plant*" (Jer. 1:10). The Holy Spirit is today in the process of uprooting and tearing down as well as building up and planting. The Lord is tearing down that which is man-made and has the attention-on-man syndrome as its foundation. He can then build a work which has Himself in the center and will carry true spiritual authority.

This is expressed in a powerful way by the prophet Zephaniah. "*Then will I purify the lips of the peoples, that all of them may call upon the name of the Lord and serve Him shoulder to shoulder.*

From beyond the rivers of Cush My worshipers, My scattered people, will bring Me offerings. On that day you will not be put to shame for all the wrongs you have done to Me, because I will remove from this city those who rejoice in their pride. Never again will you be haughty on My holy hill. But I will leave within you the meek and the humble, who trust in the name of the Lord. The remnant of Israel will do no wrong; they will speak no lies, nor will deceit be found in their mouths. They will eat and lie down and no one will make them afraid" (Zeph. 3:9–13). This prophecy speaks of the restoration of the nation of Israel as well as the work of salvation through Christ. But it is also a specific message which the Holy Spirit brings to the Church today to instruct her in the ways of the Lord for this time.

In His work to tear down and uproot, the Lord will *"remove from this city those who rejoice in their pride."* There is extensive pride within God's "city," the Church, today. Just like with Jesus' disciples, there is frequent discussion of who is the greatest, either in plain words or in between the lines. Just like within the Corinthian church, there are constant group formations around certain leaders and systems, hindering the oneness of the whole Body of Christ. Much of this has its roots in pride, where we become prideful of ourselves or others. We take pride in belonging to a part of the Body which appears to be more successful than other parts. We take pride in being more doctrinally correct than others. We take pride in following leaders who have a greater VIP/celebrity standing than others. We take pride in the use of great natural talent, our own or that of others. There are simply many areas where pride is a driving force which puts the Church in a stumbling mode. *"Pride goes before destruction, a haughty spirit before a fall"* (Prov. 16:18).

The Church has been stumbling and falling all over the place. Not just because the enemy so forcefully attacked but because of its own pride. A humble Church can withstand any attack from the enemy. A prideful Church falls by its own weight. God

is today dealing with this problem by removing such an attitude from His "city." This is why our willingness to confront
the attention-on-man syndrome is so important.

We need to mention another form of pride as well. Although
not related to this specific area of teaching, this type of pride still
has great impact on the Church's ability to walk a balanced walk.
*"Love not the world, neither the things that are in the world. If
any man love the world, the love of the Father is not in him. For
all that is in the world, the lust of the flesh, and the lust of the
eyes, and the pride of life, is not of the Father, but is of the world"*
(1 John 2:15–16 King James). The pride of life — undue focus on
material wealth, human intelligence, natural talent, good looks,
appearance of one's body, superior education, position in society,
etc. — is a common sin within the Church. So much so, that there
is even certain Christian teaching that flat out elevates these
things to a completely wrongful level. God is in the process of
removing this type of pride from His people as well. The time
has come for the Church to be filled with inner strength, inner
beauty and spiritual wisdom and understanding. Not the outward attributes which might be good for television coverage and
bold newspaper headlines but has little to do with true spirituality. The gospel of the cross is truly foolishness to the
unregenerated mind and will never make it into the world of
wealth and beauty.

God continues through Zephaniah: *"Never again will you be
haughty on My holy hill."* Haughtiness is basically pride with an
arrogant twist. The haughtiness within the Church is obvious to
those who would allow the Spirit to open their eyes. Sometimes it
is even called "faith" or "spiritual authority." Haughtiness occurs
basically when we accept the idea that we are to use God and His
promises for our benefit, rather than letting God apply His word
on us in order to use us for His benefit. There is a world of difference between these two attitudes. Haughtiness hinders true fear
of God which in turn results in the lack of spiritual wisdom and

authority. God is today working to remove this sin from among His people. Never again should we be haughty on His holy hill, the Church.

Many Christians rejoice in pride and haughtiness. There is great evidence of this in different areas. The main proof that pride and haughtiness are accepted in the Church—indeed, not only accepted but literally "rejoiced" over—is the attention-on-man syndrome. The Lord makes it very clear to His people today that He is going to have no more of this. If we do not willingly change our hearts and give up this attitude, He will Himself forcefully remove it. God desires a Church which can be the object of His wonderful grace. He is no longer satisfied with one where He often times even has to be its active opponent. *"God opposes the proud but gives grace to the humble"* (1 Peter 5:5). In fact, God will likely more and more fulfill this promise of His opposition to the proud among His people, (yes, this is a Scripture promise, too!), in order to achieve His goal to purify the Church.

As the Holy Spirit tears down the sin of pride and haughtiness, He plants and builds something new. *"But I will leave within you the meek and the humble."* This is the framework of the true Church in the end times: the meek and humble. As the Church proceeds into final battle with the enemy, this is the only army that will stand. The pride and haughtiness of the flesh act like magnets pulling in the fiery darts of the enemy. But the meek and the humble in spirit can't be touched. They are free from the attitude that would invite and then crumble under enemy attack.

There are three additional characteristics of the meek and humble in this prophecy. First, they are the ones *"who trust in the name of the Lord."* This will be the only name of importance in a triumphant Church. Jesus is the only name that one should trust in. Not the names of human beings, no matter who they are. The focus will be completely on the name of the Lord and the attention-on-man syndrome will be put aside.

Secondly, *"they will speak no lies, nor will deceit be found in their mouths."* The honesty and openness of the true Church will be staggering. No longer will we try to impress each other by putting a "makeup" face on different works, employing the correct PR around our ministry, major on the positive so that people will have a good feeling, beef-up our statistics so that it would make our service for God look a little better. Or whatever else we are doing in the name of faith or positiveness, which many times is nothing but deceit anyway. God is not pleased with this and will see to it that it is removed from His Church. He has not instructed us to think either positive with some kind of an over-drive faith approach, or negative with a radical but in reality judgmental and often unloving spirit. God desires for us to be *truthful*, which is sometimes positive, sometimes negative. We should express whatever the truth is. This must be the trademark of the end-time Church.

Thirdly, *"No one will make them afraid."* There will be no fear in such a Church. Fear is basically a concern of losing that which is important to us; our life, our provision, our position, etc. However, when Christ has become our everything, we have nothing to lose and thus nothing to fear. The attention-on-man syndrome has great influence here. If we are focused on human strength and ability—our own or others'—and view man in an incorrect role within the Church, we will never be free from fear. On the other hand, if we put full attention on Jesus, all fear is gone.

The Lord takes great delight in the true worshipers who occupy His holy hill. He continues to speak through Zephaniah: *"The Lord your God is with you, He is mighty to save. He will take great delight in you, He will quiet you with His love, He will rejoice over you with singing"* (Zeph. 3:17). Can you hear God's heart sing as He rejoices over the meek and humble? Can you recognize a pure, heavenly melody sounding over those who have put their trust in the name of the Lord only? Can you sense the awesome power

and might of God as He works through those who have repented
from the sin of pride and haughtiness?

The Restored City, the victorious Church, will be glorious and
powerful. The true Body of Christ will proudly lift its Head high
for all the world to see the beauty and power of Christ—no one
else. Its leadership will not be faceless or nameless, but will see
itself only as a conduit for the authority and leadership of Christ.
Indeed, the only useful leadership will be that which deliberately
renounces a man-pleasing attitude. Paul addresses this strongly in
1 Thessalonians. "*We are not trying to please men but God, who
tests our hearts. You know we never used flattery, nor did we put on
a mask to cover up greed—God is our witness. We were not looking
for praise from men, not from you or anyone else*" (1 Thess. 2:4–6).
And the flock will view its shepherds as channels of Christ's leadership only. Not be infatuated with the shepherds' own standing.

The Restored City is called to be an "equal opportunity" estab-
lishment. There will be no racism, differences of class, or other
expressions of certain humans being perceived to be better or
higher than others. The unity of the Spirit through the bond of
love will ensure this. All worship and praise—as well as applause
and hurrays—will go to the Lord in awesome recognition of the
work of Christ. Not to man because of position or special ability
God may have given him in His work. The restored Church will
not be driven by the attention-on-man syndrome, but rather by
the Holy Spirit calling, sending, and gathering with complete
focus on Christ. The members of the Body will seek and know
each other not "*after the flesh, but after the Spirit*" (Rom. 8:4 KJV),
i.e., not based on natural attributes, human talent, fame, etc., but
focused on the life and work of Christ in each member, well-known
or not. Thus, there will be less attention given to natural abilities
and visible position.

A great time of service lies ahead for the Church in God's plan.
Will the Lord find a meek and humble people to move with Him?
Zephaniah prophesied that the people with purified lips would

serve the Lord *"shoulder to shoulder."* The *"shoulder to shoulder"*-Church is being called together worldwide right now by the Holy Spirit. It is being prepared for a major move of God at the end of the age. This Church will walk in true fear of God—not men. And it stands in awe of Christ—not His servants. It rises up in a shout of victory with major emphasis on strength, honor, glory, and praise. Not to itself, but to Him who sits on the throne and to the Lamb.